In association with

United Nations Children's Fund

# A life like mine

DK Publishing

LONDON, NEW YORK, MUNICH,
MELBOURNE, AND DELHI

**UNICEF (NY) Consultant** Arati Rao
**Senior Editor** Amanda Rayner
**Senior Art Editor** Claire Penny
**Project Editor** Zahavit Shalev
**Art Editors** Laura Roberts, Venice Shone
**Researcher** Lisa Magloff
**Design Assistant** Abbie Collinson

**Design Consultant** Jane Bull
**Managing Editor** Sue Leonard
**Managing Art Editor** Cathy Chesson
**Category Publisher** Mary Ling
**US Editors** Margaret Parrish, Jennifer Siklós
**Picture Research** Angela Anderson, Sarah Pownall
**Jacket Design** Sophia Tampakopoulos
**Production** Silvia La Greca Bertacchi,
Shivani Pandey
**DTP Designer** Almudena Díaz

All maps used in this book are artistic representations.
They do not reflect a position by UNICEF or Dorling Kindersley on the
legal status of any country or territory or the delimitation of any frontiers.
Dotted line represents approximately the Line of Control in Jammu and Kashmir
agreed upon by India and Pakistan. The final status of Jammu and
Kashmir has not yet been agreed upon by the parties.

Every effort has been made to ensure that the statistics in this book are up to date
at the time of going to press.

First American Edition, 2002
02 03 04 05 10 9 8 7 6 5 4 3

Published in the United States by
DK Publishing, Inc.
375 Hudson Street
New York, New York 10014

**Library of Congress Cataloging-in-Publication Data**
A life like mine
    p. cm.
"In association with UNICEF, United Nations Children's Fund."
Summary: Looks at what life is like for children of different countries and how
easily each child can fulfill his or her hopes and ambitions no matter how little
or far their human rights are infringed.
  ISBN 0-7894-8859-0
  1. Children's rights--Cross-cultural studies--Juvenile literature. 2. Children--
Cross-cultural studies--Juvenile literature. [1. Children's rights. 2. Children.]
I. UNICEF.
  HQ789 .L54 2002
  305.23--dc21
                                                    2002011197

Color reproduction by GRB Editrice, S.r.l., Verona
Printed and bound by Mondadori Printing S.p.A., Verona, Italy

See our complete
product line at
www.dk.com

# unicef
## United Nations Children's Fund

There are millions of children, leading different lives, all over the world. You speak different languages, look different, and face all kinds of challenges every day. However, although you live thousands of miles apart, in many respects your needs and hopes are alike.

It is for this reason that the Convention on the Rights of the Child has been drawn up and accepted by almost every country of the world. It promises essential rights to every one of the world's children. Each child, boys and girls equally, has a right to education, health care, food, shelter, play, and protection – and much more.

*A Life Like Mine* records the courage, energy, joy, and optimism of children from all over the world. Some of the children in this book enjoy every privilege in their lives; others have been deprived of some of their basic rights. I hope you enjoy meeting them and that you discover the similarities between their lives and your own.

You are special. You deserve protection and support as you grow to adulthood. You are part of the present, but all of the future.

Harry Belafonte, Goodwill Ambassador for UNICEF

――――――― About UNICEF ―――――――

UNICEF's mission is to create conditions that enable children to live happy, healthy, and dignified lives.
Every aspect of UNICEF's work – ranging from programs to improve children's health and education to protecting children from violence, exploitation, and disasters – is guided by the Convention on the Rights of the Child.

**www.unicef.org**

# 1. Survival

 # 2. Development

 # 3. Protection

 # 4. Participation

# Contents

# Where do they live?

In this book you will meet children from around the world. Although they seem very different, they all share one goal – they want to lead a good life. In the following pages you'll learn about their lives, thoughts, and hopes for the future.

## Natalie

Natalie is nine years old. She lives in Bedfordshire, England. Meet her on page 42.

## Taralyn

Taralyn is 10 years old. She lives near Seattle, Washington. Meet Taralyn on page 120.

**UNITED STATES**

## Isa

Isa is 10 years old. He lives in Sierra Leone. Meet him on page 88.

## C.J.

C.J. is 13 years old. He lives in Atlanta, Georgia. Meet C.J. on page 96.

**COLOMBIA**

### Children around the World

There are over six billion people in the world. More than two billion of them are under 18.

More than 210 million children of ages 5–14 work. More than half of those are involved in dangerous work or work full-time.

Nearly 11 million children under five die each year, mostly from preventable diseases.

## Mayerly

Mayerly is 18. She lives in Bogotá, Colombia. Meet her on page 126.

## Ivana

Ivana is 12 years old. She lives in Pristina, Yugoslavia. Meet her on page 72.

## Eli

Eli is 15. He lives at Yemin Orde Youth Village in Israel. Meet him on page 112.

## Nadin

Nadin is 11. She lives in the Kalandia camp in the Occupied Palestinian Territory. Meet her on page 34.

## Najaha & Abdisukri

Najaha is 10 and Abdisukri is nine. They live in Tilburg, Netherlands. Meet them on page 108.

## Maria

Maria is nine. She lives in Kabul, Afghanistan. Meet her on page 54.

UK

**NETHERLANDS**

**YUGOSLAVIA**

**ISRAEL AND OCCUPIED PALESTINIAN TERRITORY**

**AFGHANISTAN**

**BANGLADESH**

**INDIA**

**LAOS**

## Nou

Nou is nine. She lives in Ponsavanh, Laos. Meet her on page 16.

**SUDAN**

**SIERRA LEONE**

## Mahasin

Mahasin is nine years old. She lives in Tambisco, Sudan. Meet her on page 32.

**RWANDA**

**SOUTH AFRICA**

**AUSTRALIA**

## Sbongile

Sbongile is 10 years old. She lives in Cape Town, South Africa. Meet her on page 52.

## Vincent

Vincent is 15 years old. He lives in Rwanda. Meet him on page 24.

## Sibasish

Sibasish is 13 years old. He lives in Kolkata, India. Meet him on page 124.

## Arif

Arif is 12. He lives in Dhaka, Bangladesh. Meet him on page 80.

## Michael

Michael is six. He lives on Lake Torrens Station in Australia. Meet him on page 62.

# 1. Survival

Every child should have **water** that is safe to drink close to their home.

Every child should have enough nourishing **food** to eat so they can grow and thrive.

Survival – noun; to survive – verb **1** to remain alive; to continue to live. **2** to continue to function or manage in spite of some adverse circumstance or hardship; hold up; endure.

# Home should be a place where
every child can feel comfortable and safe.

Every child should have access to **health** care in order to lead a full and active life.

Every child should have

# Water

bathing, ceremony, drinking,

# The water of life

Without water, there would be no life on Earth.
Water is our planet's most precious possession.
A human being can survive only a few days without water.
We use water in so many different ways without even thinking about it. Some of us just turn the faucet on and water gushes out. But not everybody in the world can take water for granted.

growing food, swimming, playing

# How much water is there?

More than 70% of the world is covered in water.

**Imagine** waking up tomorrow to find that there were no faucets. **What would you do?**

• **Like many people** in the world, you would have to get the water you needed from a river, lake, well, pump, or communal faucet.

• **Water keeps us alive.** We use it to drink, to grow food, and to bathe. It's also essential for building houses and running factories.

• **About 97 percent of the world's water is salty** seawater and cannot be used. Most of the freshwater in the world is too difficult to reach because it's underground or in icebergs. Only 1 percent of the Earth's freshwater is available – but that's still plenty for our needs.

## How much **water** do you use?

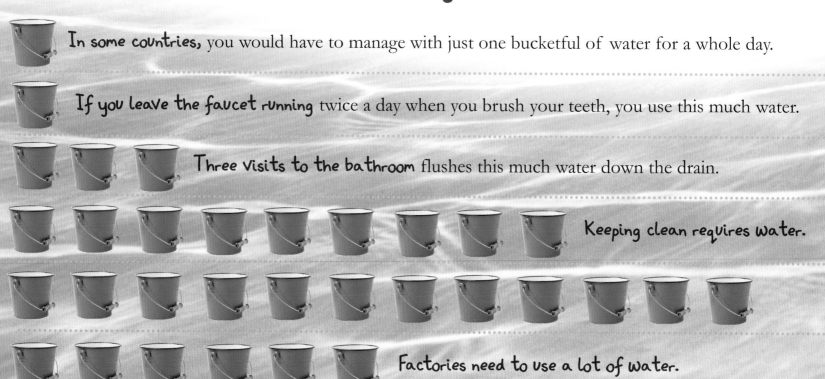

**In some countries,** you would have to manage with just one bucketful of water for a whole day.

**If you leave the faucet running** twice a day when you brush your teeth, you use this much water.

**Three visits to the bathroom** flushes this much water down the drain.

Keeping clean requires water.

Factories need to use a lot of water.

Even the 1 percent of freshwater available on our planet is sometimes unsafe to drink.

# So is there enough water for everyone?
## Yes! But there are still problems...

• **Too little rain** Enough rainwater falls every day to cover the land in a layer 31 in (80 cm) deep. That should be plenty for everyone. The problem is that more rain falls in some areas than in others.

• **Bad water** Every day 14,000 people die because the water they use contains dangerous chemicals or untreated sewage. Diarrhea, caused by dirty water and dirty conditions, kills more than 1 million children a year.

• **Too much rain** Many fertile parts of the world are prone to flooding. Floods destroy people's homes and often cause the water supply to become dirty. This makes it easy for diseases to spread.

• **Dry deserts** 14 percent of the world's surface is desert, and the desert is growing all the time. Deserts have little or no rainfall. People have to walk miles to get water for themselves, their animals, and their crops.

## Water facts

Believe it or not, 75 percent of you is water!

You would probably die after three days without water.

Water makes up 50 percent of your bones.

That means water for **drinking**, **bathing**, and **cooking**.

That's **a whole day's supply** for some people.

= 2.6 gallons (10 liters)

This much water **fills a bathtub**.

**Washing machines** guzzle all this water for one load of laundry.

We can't drink seawater because it's too salty.

It took this amount of water to make **the shoes you are wearing**.

# Watery tales

These children are lucky to have access to clean, safe running water. Yet most of them have to get it daily for their families – a difficult and time-consuming task.

**Afghanistan** Two boys get water from a hand pump. Villages in this region are affected by drought, so these pumps are a lifeline. Local people have received hygiene education and have been trained in maintaining the hand pumps.

This village in Afghanistan was bombed during a war in the 1980s. Even in 2002 it had still not been rebuilt.

A bucket to carry the water home

**India** Two girls carry containers to a communal water source. They will fill them up with water and then take them home. The girls use as many containers as they can for each trip, and carry the biggest pots on their heads and the other containers in their hands. Their heads are cushioned from the metal pots by a piece of cloth.

• • • A 2.6-gallon (10-liter) bucket of water weighs 22 lb (10 kg). That's very heavy. In fact, it's about the same weight as a one-year-old child!

**The Netherlands** Najaha helps herself to a glass of water from the faucet in her kitchen. She's the only person on this page who doesn't have to leave her house to get water.

• • • How many faucets and sinks are there in your home? How would your life change if there were only one faucet in your home? What if you had to collect water from outside your home? Or from a few streets away?

**Jamaica** A girl fills a bucket with water from a community standpipe. The standpipe is not as convenient as having a faucet in your house, but it's better than having to get water from a river or a lake. When people come to collect their water, they also share news and gossip.

• • • Before it reaches the standpipe, the water is pumped out of the ground. Then it must be treated to remove dirt and germs so it will be safe to drink. Otherwise, it is no safer than river water.

Water gushes out!

# Nou

Two years ago, a pump was installed in Nou's village in Laos. Previously, people collected water from a stream. It was not safe and often made them sick.

### BEFORE THE PUMP

A nearby stream provided all the water for Nou's village. The water was not safe, but it was all the villagers had. For three months of the year, the stream dried up. People dug into the streambed for water, but it was always muddy.

.... "Now that there is safe water to drink, people have stopped getting sick and can spend less time and money on visits to the doctor."

### GETTING WATER

Children in Laos get water for their families. Nou and her friends used to make many trips to the stream, sometimes missing school.

### Laos

Mountainous and full of forests, Laos has a monsoon climate. This means both droughts and floods occur, depending on the season.

"I had my own buckets, which were smaller than the ones my older sister used."

## THE TRIP

The walk to get water included a steep hill and a rickety bridge. It took 10 minutes to get there, but 20 minutes returning with heavy buckets.

 "I used to get water from the stream twice a day. I would walk with my friends. We could talk while we went even though the buckets were heavy."

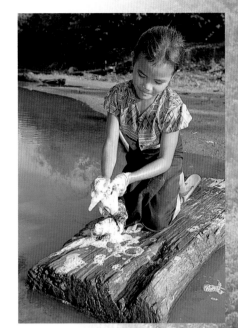

## MORE TIME

Now that the pump is in the center of the village, everyone has more time than before – Nou to play, and her mother to help in the fields.

"We can get water so easily. I can go and bring back a fresh bucket whenever I want."

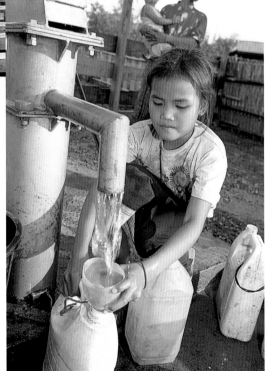

## LAUNDRY

People still use the river to do laundry, but going to the bathroom is simpler and more hygienic, thanks to a new covered toilet built by Nou's father and brother.

"The roof and walls of our bathroom are made of leaves and thatch, and it's not far from the house."

## SCHOOL GARDEN

The village has a new feature now. A garden was impractical before because it was too far to go to get water for the plants. That is not a problem now because the village pump is actually in the school yard.

 "We have a school garden with flowers in it. We water it every day."

"Life is better now!"

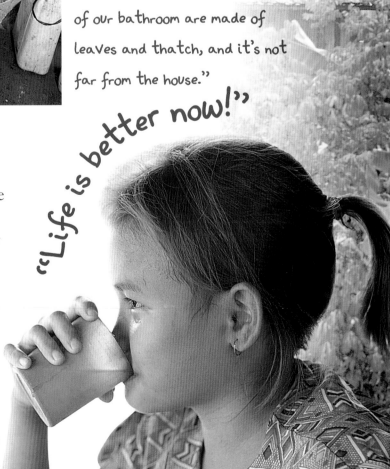

Every child should have

# food

survival, growth, good health,

# Food is our fuel

We eat in order to survive.

We enjoy the tastes, smells, and textures of food.

Most celebrations and holidays involve eating together.

While people in rich parts of the world are dying from diseases caused by overeating, many in poorer parts of the world are struggling just to get enough food to survive.

# strength, energy, feasting

# Why do we need food?

Every day, 14% of people in the world go to bed hungry.

14%

**Have you** ever tried to study or play when you were **hungry?**

• **When children don't get enough food**, they don't have the energy to work, play, or learn. Their bodies and brains don't grow as well as they should, and they are more likely to suffer from diseases.

• **Malnutrition** means not getting enough of the food you need. Every year, millions of children die from diseases made worse by malnutrition.

• **When there is a shortage of food**, some parents in some countries will feed their sons better than their daughters, resulting in worse malnutrition among girls.

Proteins

## What happens when we do not eat a balanced diet?

One child in four does not get enough **protein** or calories.

Filling foods like rice, noodles, bread, and cereals are called **carbohydrates.**

One person in two does not get enough **vitamins** and **minerals.**

Foods containing **sugars** and **fats** can taste really good.

Vitamins and minerals

### Eat good food!

# Why do people go hungry?

- **Environmental problems**, such as drought, floods, and deforestation, destroy the soil, making it hard to grow food. Problems get worse when people farm land with damaged soil.

- **War** forces people away from their homes and off their land, so it's hard to plant crops and distribute food that is grown. During war, governments spend money on weapons instead of food.

- **Overgrazing** by animals damages the land and the soil, so crops cannot grow. Overfishing affects not just the number of fish in the ocean, but other animals and plants in the food chain.

- **Some people don't have money** to buy all the food they need, or enough land and tools to grow it themselves. As food becomes less available, the price goes up even more.

## A good idea?

Why can't we just send hungry people our extra food?

It would stop people from dying, but it wouldn't solve the reasons why hunger happens.

Governments need to make sure that everyone has a way to grow or buy the food they need.

Many poor people have to spend almost all of their money on food, leaving very little left over for other necessities.

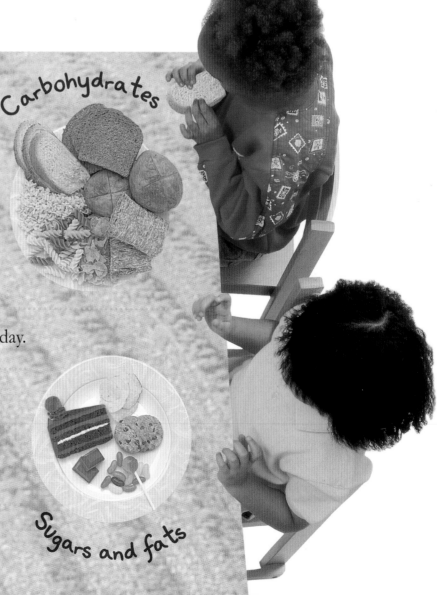

Carbohydrates

Each child is sick for **many days** each year.

Without them, children have **no energy** to get through the day.

This **weakens** the body's resistance to **disease**.

But too much can make us **overweight** and **unhealthy**.

## Stay healthy and happy!

Sugars and fats

# What's cooking?

A staple food is the one that our meals are based around. Whether it's bread, rice, noodles, or potatoes, when we see or smell it we know we won't be hungry for long.

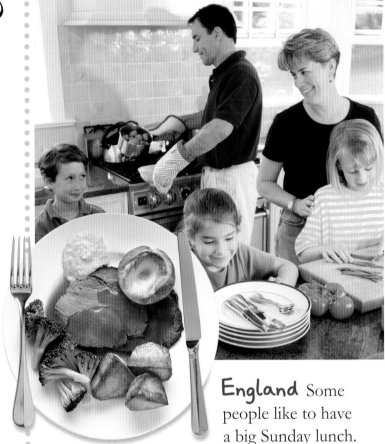

**England** Some people like to have a big Sunday lunch. A traditional main course for this meal might consist of roast beef, roast potatoes, Yorkshire pudding, vegetables, and gravy.

● ● ● This meal is eaten at a table using knives and forks. English people often chat during a big meal.

**Viet Nam** There are lots of rivers and lakes in Southeast Asia, so people eat plenty of fish.

● ● ● In Asia, most meals contain either rice or noodles. Vietnamese people eat food from a bowl using chopsticks.

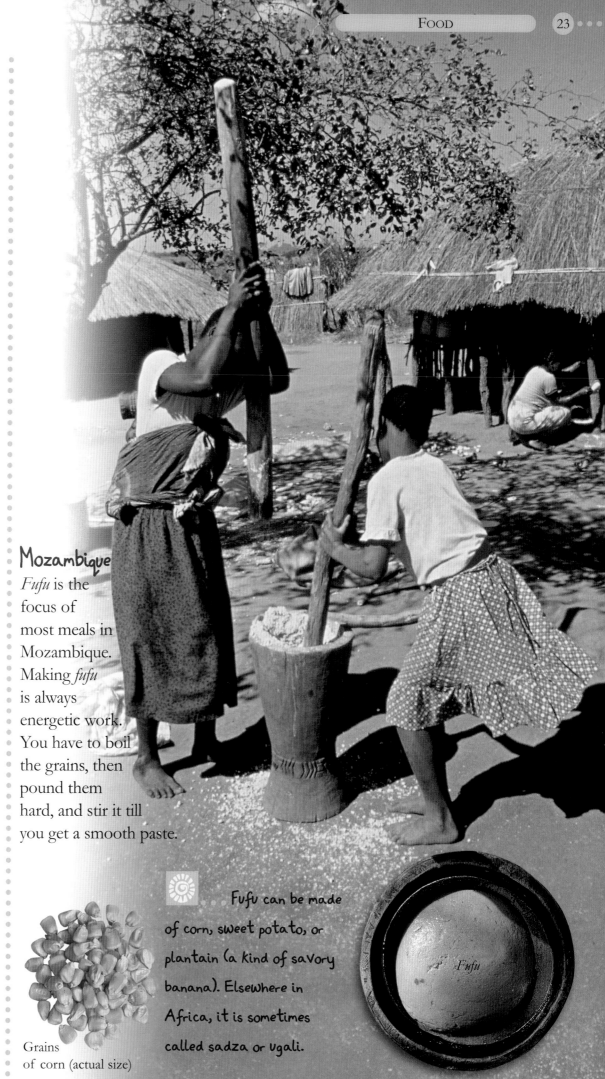

## Bangladesh
Typical flavorings for food include salt, coriander, turmeric, cumin, chilli powder, garlic, onions, and chilies.

... In Bangladesh, people eat using only their right hand. People don't talk much while they eat.

## Mozambique
*Fufu* is the focus of most meals in Mozambique. Making *fufu* is always energetic work. You have to boil the grains, then pound them hard, and stir it till you get a smooth paste.

... Fufu can be made of corn, sweet potato, or plantain (a kind of savory banana). Elsewhere in Africa, it is sometimes called sadza or ugali.

Grains of corn (actual size)

*Fufu*

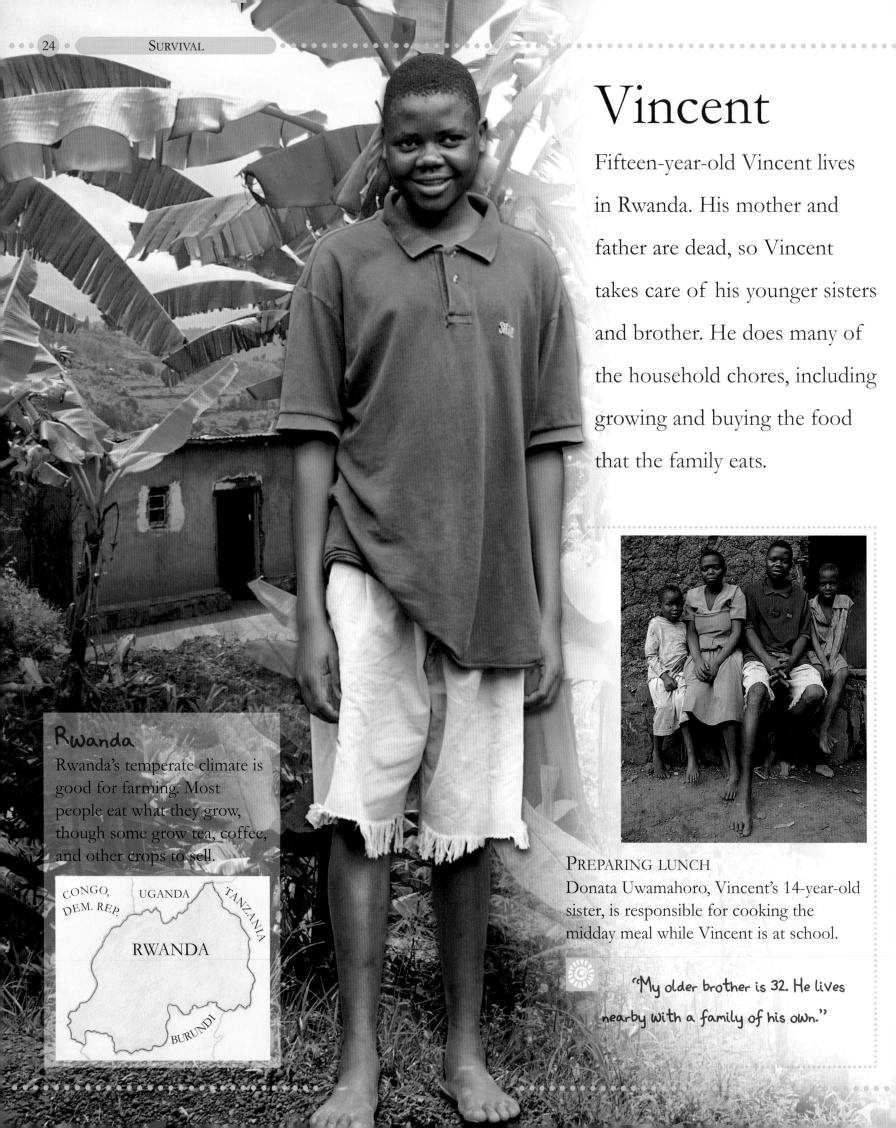

# Vincent

Fifteen-year-old Vincent lives in Rwanda. His mother and father are dead, so Vincent takes care of his younger sisters and brother. He does many of the household chores, including growing and buying the food that the family eats.

## Rwanda

Rwanda's temperate climate is good for farming. Most people eat what they grow, though some grow tea, coffee, and other crops to sell.

PREPARING LUNCH
Donata Uwamahoro, Vincent's 14-year-old sister, is responsible for cooking the midday meal while Vincent is at school.

"My older brother is 32. He lives nearby with a family of his own."

## BANANAS AND GOATS

Vincent grows bananas on his land. He also keeps some goats in an enclosure. They provide manure for the crops.

... "I get up when it is light. I don't have a watch. My first task is to cut some grass to feed to our goats."

## VEGETABLE PATCH

Vincent's brother helps him weed the cabbage patch. A local organization gave Vincent advice about growing vegetables, so he also grows tomatoes and sweet potatoes.

... "We used to earn a little from our coffee bushes, but they have stopped producing beans. I make money from doing odd jobs now."

## WORKING WITH WOOD

Vincent takes carpentry lessons at a day center for orphans run by a local organization.

... "I wish to become a carpenter so that I can earn a living by making beds and other furniture."

## ALL FIRED UP

Vincent's sister does most of the cooking, but her brothers help her light the fire.

"We have one meal a day. I eat at school, the others eat at home."

# Every child should have a

# home

## Warm, cool, dry, safe, shelter,

# Home sweet home

Our homes protect us from the weather.
At home, we feel safe, comfortable, and relaxed.
A home can be built anywhere and out of anything.
Around the world, people live in all kinds of homes
including houses, apartments, campers, caves,
houseboats, treehouses, and tents.

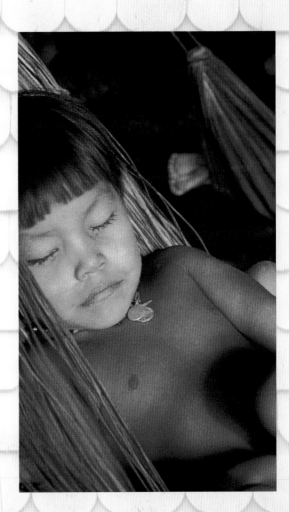

privacy, space, comfort, peace

# Where do people live?

**A home** is more than a building. It is a place where you can be **secure**, **safe**, **healthy**, and **happy**.

It doesn't matter what a house looks like, but to be a good home for children, a house needs to provide:

- **Protection** from the weather, injury, smoke, and pollution;
- **A safe water supply** in the house or nearby;
- **Sturdy walls** that cannot catch fire easily;
- **Sanitary ways** to get rid of human waste and garbage;
- **Safe food storage** and preparation;
- **Enough room** for everyone living there;
- **Adults** who can care for children.

## There is not **enough** affordable housing,

**Nearly half** of the world's population lives in cities.

**250 million** people in cities do not have safe piped water.

**400 million** people in cities have no toilet or latrine.

At least **600 million** people live in city slums or shantytowns.

More than 20 million families in the world's cities are homeless.

Not everyone is homeless for the same reason.
There are many causes of homelessness.

- **War and violence** force people out of their homes. Over half of the world's refugees are children. Some children run away from home because of violence.

- When there is **no work**, people leave the country and move to the cities. This makes the cities very crowded, and housing there is even more expensive.

- **Natural disasters**, such as droughts, floods, volcanos, and storms, can destroy homes. After a disaster, there might not be any money to rebuild houses.

- **There is not enough cheap housing** for all the people who need it. The unemployed or those earning very little sometimes end up on the streets.

### There are lots of different kinds of houses

In the hot deserts of Tunisia, some people live in underground houses, where it is cool.

On the rivers of Hong Kong and Thailand, people sometimes live on riverboats.

## so some people have to **live** in bad conditions.

- A third of all city dwellers live in substandard housing.

- That means the poorest families have nowhere to bathe. Many have to buy water from expensive water sellers.

- Many families have to share a bathroom. They face a bleak future, exposed to conditions that breed disease.

- **1.3 billion** people have inadequate housing.

# A place to live

Homes differ enormously around the world. There are city homes and country homes, homes in hot climates and in cold climates, homes on or near water, and homes on or near mountains. What makes a home a home? The people who live in it.

**Turkey** Our earliest ancestors probably found shelter from the sun, wind, and rain in caves. Today, some people still choose to live in a cave or to use a cave as the basis for their houses. This home is built into the side of a cave. The thick walls help keep the home cool in summer and warm in winter.

... The most convenient thing about a cave dwelling is that you don't have to build your home from scratch because the cave is already there.

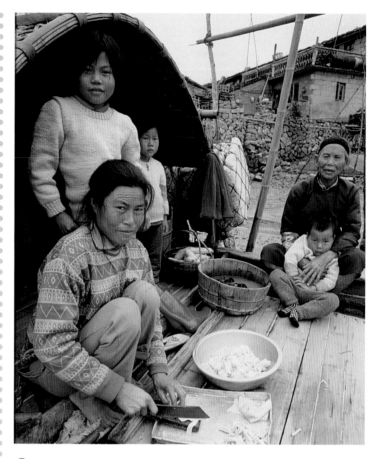

**China** A family sits in their wooden houseboat moored in the shallows near a fishing village in Fujian Province. Living on the river is practical both for fishing and for selling the fish you catch, so it's often fishermen and their families who live in homes like these.

... When you live on a houseboat, you get used to the slight rocking motion of the water and the cramped conditions. Children brought up on a houseboat learn to swim and to behave responsibly around the water from an early age.

**Laos** People in Laos weave panels out of rattan (a kind of grass). It only takes one day for the panels to be lashed together to form a house. However, the panels do need to be replaced regularly.

... In the rainy season, it can get very muddy. That's why this house is built on stilts. The area on the right is a pen where the family keeps their pigs. The pigs don't mind the mud!

**England** TJ's family works in a traveling circus in England. They are on the road for most of the year. They live in this trailer, which they bought in the US. It is very comfortable and has a washing machine and a microwave.

... The children of people who travel go to many different schools. They keep a record book that they take to each school.

**Rwanda** Vincent lives here with his two sisters and his brother. Their two-room house is made of sunbaked mud brick. Vincent and his family built their own house, with help from their neighbors and friends, who pitched in to make bricks and construct the house.

... When there is no money for expensive building materials, people use whatever materials are available. Thick mud bricks are practical in hot, dry climates because they keep the house cool.

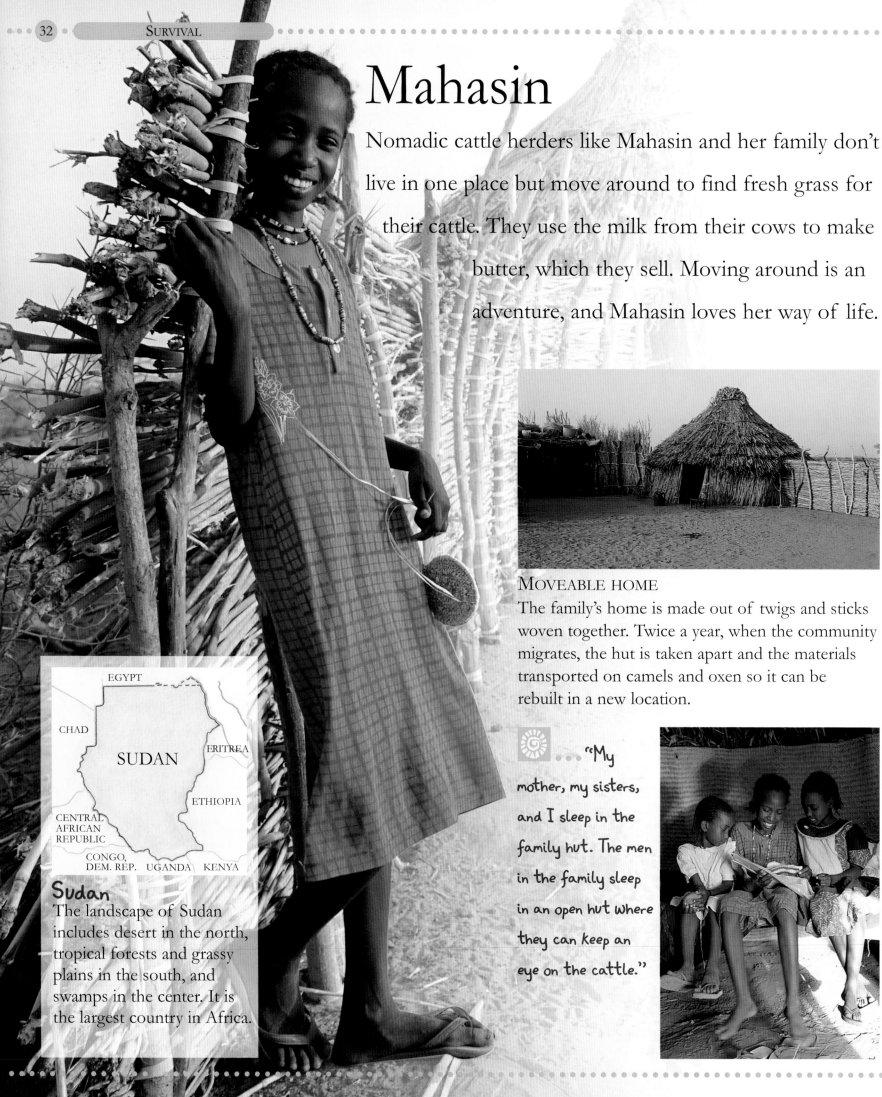

# Mahasin

Nomadic cattle herders like Mahasin and her family don't live in one place but move around to find fresh grass for their cattle. They use the milk from their cows to make butter, which they sell. Moving around is an adventure, and Mahasin loves her way of life.

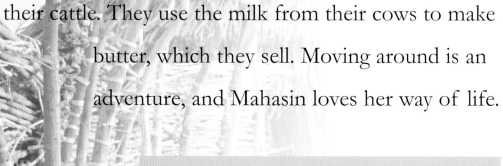

## MOVEABLE HOME
The family's home is made out of twigs and sticks woven together. Twice a year, when the community migrates, the hut is taken apart and the materials transported on camels and oxen so it can be rebuilt in a new location.

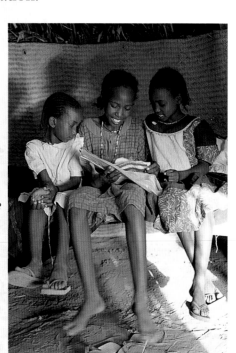

... "My mother, my sisters, and I sleep in the family hut. The men in the family sleep in an open hut where they can keep an eye on the cattle."

## Sudan
The landscape of Sudan includes desert in the north, tropical forests and grassy plains in the south, and swamps in the center. It is the largest country in Africa.

EGYPT

CHAD

SUDAN

ERITREA

ETHIOPIA

CENTRAL AFRICAN REPUBLIC

CONGO, DEM. REP. UGANDA KENYA

## NOMADIC LIFE

Mahasin's family moves frequently in order to find grass and water for their cattle. All of Mahasin's personal belongings need to fit into one small trunk.

... "The thing I like best in life is when we move. Wherever we go with our cattle, people treat us with respect and often help us. We can go everywhere we want."

## STAPLE FOOD

Mahasin likes to help her mother and sisters with the cooking and cleaning. The family's staple food is called *asida*. It is a dish of vegetables and grains mixed with spices.

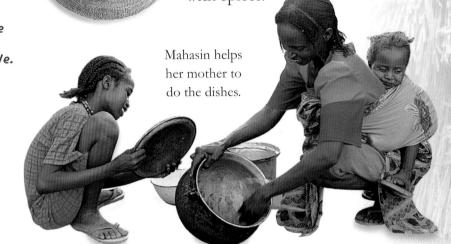

Mahasin helps her mother to do the dishes.

## TRAVELING SCHOOL

Mahasin attends a special school for nomadic children. There are about 50 children at the school, but students change all the time because of constant migrations.

... "We learn the Arabic language, religion, and geography. Our teacher's name is Fadul Osman. He always travels with us. He is one of us."

## BASKETWEAVING

When Mahasin is not studying, she helps her family to take care of their cattle and weaves baskets for the family to use.

Mahasin's necklace is called a *khannakh*.

## A DESERT HOPPING GAME

Mahasin and her friends play a traditional game called *arikkia*.

# Nadin

Nadin and her family live in a refugee camp in the West Bank run by the United Nations. Her family fled from their original town of Malha, historical Palestine, after the 1948 Arab-Israeli war.

### A FAMILY HOME

Nadin, her parents, two sisters, and a brother all live on just the lower floor of the house. Nadin's grandparents, aunt, uncle, and their children all live on the upper floor.

... "My family has been living in the camp for more than 53 years, since it was set up in 1949. My grandmother was six when she moved here from the town of Malha."

### AT PLAY

There are few places in the camp for girls to play, so Nadin plays either indoors or on the street in front of the house.

WEST BANK

GAZA

ISRAEL

JORDAN

EGYPT

## Occupied Palestinian Territory

The Occupied Palestinian Territory is in two separate parts – the West Bank and Gaza. Israel occupied the land during the 1967 war.

## TIME FOR BED
Nadin shares her bedroom with eight-year-old Wafa. The rest of the family sleeps in the family room.

🌀 ···· "I love my sister Wafa though we argue a lot because she is very talkative. She wants to be famous and appear on TV."

Nadin and her sister Wafa and brother Mohammed

## FAMILY TIES
Nadin is very close to everyone in her family. Because she is the eldest, she helps her mother take care of her younger sister, Hala, who is only two years old.

🌀 ···· "We eat a popular Palestinian dish called musakhan. It is made of bread, onion, chicken, and spices all fried up together."

*Musakhan*

Olives

## HELPING AT HOME
After she gets home from school, Nadin helps her mother with chores such as sweeping the floor and dusting the furniture.

## NOT SO DIFFERENT
Palestinian food is similar to that of other countries in the region, including Jordan, Israel, Turkey, Greece, Iran, and Iraq.

🌀 ···· "My biggest wish is to go back to Malha, our original city. I also wish for peace between Israelis and Palestinians."

# Every child deserves a
# healthy life

## strong bones, healthy teeth,

# Staying Well

It's best not to get sick in the first place.
Vaccinations can protect us against some diseases.
Good hygiene and a healthy diet can help us avoid others.
But sometimes people get sick. When that happens,
they may need the help of doctors, medicine, and
hospitals to get well again.

# fitness, hygiene, immunization

# What do you need to stay healthy?

**Good health** is the most precious thing you have.

- **To stay healthy**, you need good food and safe water, somewhere to bathe yourself, a place to go to the bathroom, vaccines, healthcare, and a way to dispose of your garbage safely.

- **When you get sick**, you need to be able to see someone, such as a doctor or a nurse or a healthcare worker, who can help you get better.

Healthy diet

Clean water + + Sanitation + Doctors + Vaccines = Healthy child

**More than a billion people have no access to medical care.**

- **Measles** kills one child every minute. You were probably **immunized** against the disease.

- You were probably immunized against a number of **easily preventable childhood diseases.**

- In Afghanistan most people have **no access to a doctor or nurse.**

- In **China**, the government trains people in remote villages to administer basic medical care.

- Children die from many diseases. **40,000 children** under the age of five die each day.

Some of the world's deadliest illnesses
can be easily and cheaply prevented.

- **Malaria** is caused by mosquitos. It affects up to 500 million people each year. Yet it can be prevented by sleeping under a mosquito net and by getting rid of mosquito breeding areas.

- **Malnutrition** affects 150 million children. It leaves them weak and unable to fight disease. Malnutrition can be prevented by having enough healthy food to eat and basic health care.

- **Diarrhea** causes dehydration, which kills more than 1 million children a year. It can be avoided by access to clean food and water. A person can be cured with an 8¢ packet of rehydration salts.

- **Measles** rarely kills healthy children. However, in developing countries, it kills nearly 1 million children each year. It can be prevented with a vaccine that costs 10¢ per dose.

### The tragedy of AIDS

In sub-Saharan Africa, millions of children have been orphaned by AIDS. Many more are having their education disrupted because their teachers are dying of the disease.

If you get **sick**, how long do you have to wait to see a **doctor?**

In Africa, **50 percent** were not.

Sadly, **34 million** children are not.

In Italy most people do.

They're called **barefoot doctors**.

**Malnutrition** is what kills them.

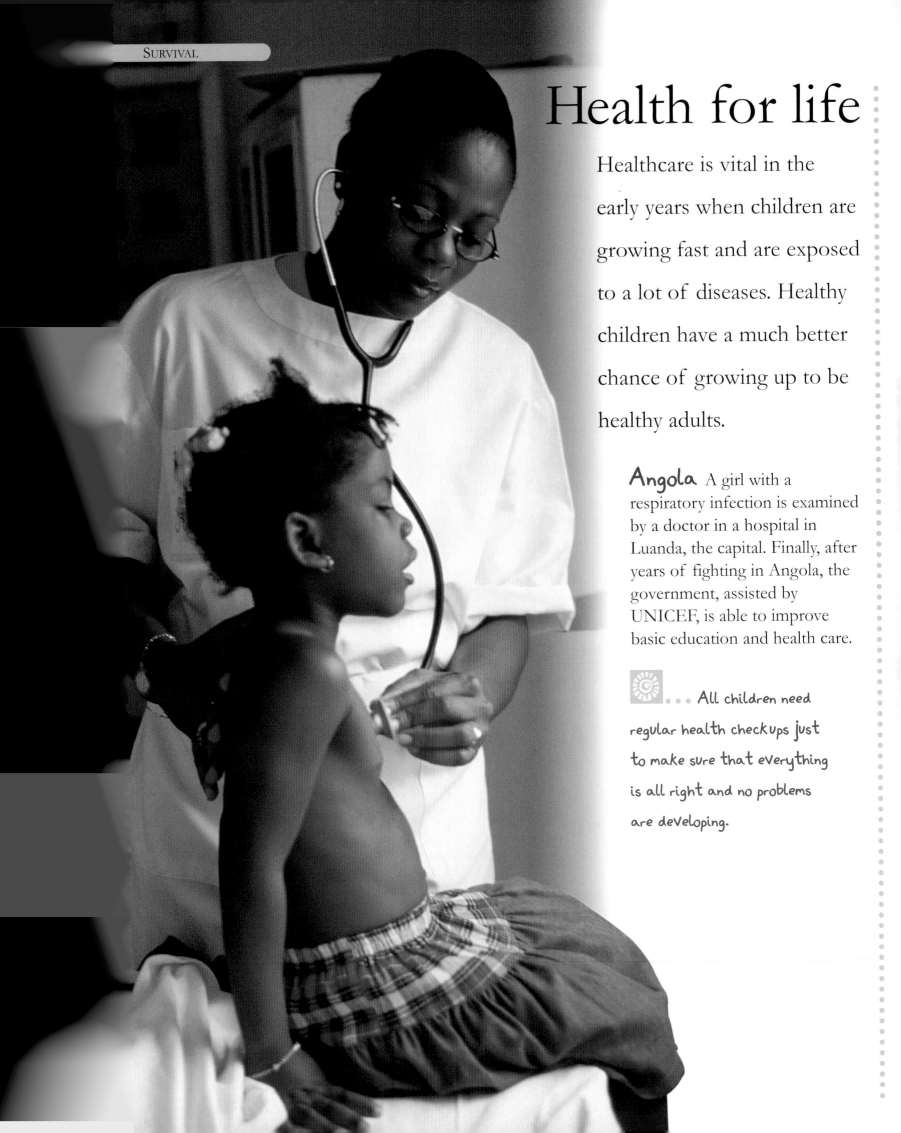

# Health for life

Healthcare is vital in the early years when children are growing fast and are exposed to a lot of diseases. Healthy children have a much better chance of growing up to be healthy adults.

**Angola** A girl with a respiratory infection is examined by a doctor in a hospital in Luanda, the capital. Finally, after years of fighting in Angola, the government, assisted by UNICEF, is able to improve basic education and health care.

... All children need regular health checkups just to make sure that everything is all right and no problems are developing.

**India** A girl smiles as she carries a clay jug of water to her home in Tamil Nadu. Sadly, dirty drinking water is responsible for many preventable deaths, especially in babies and young children.

... Pots like these keep water fresh and cool. However, a safe supply of tap water would be much more convenient for everyone.

**Bangladesh** This two-year-old girl has plenty to smile about as she splashes clean bath water. The bath water in her plastic basin came from a new hand pump.

... Using a river or lake for bathing or for going to the bathroom makes the water unsafe for drinking.

**Zambia** Fruits and vegetables are rich in vitamins and minerals that help us recover from diseases, and even prevent us from getting sick in the first place. Different foods contain different nutrients, so it's important to have a balanced diet.

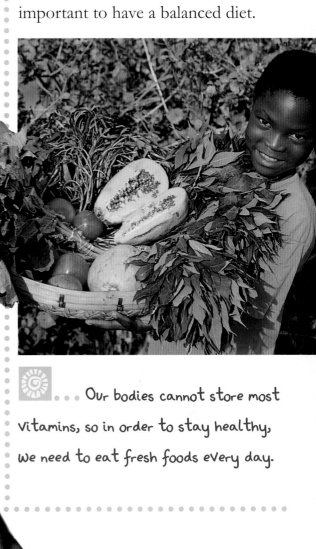

... Our bodies cannot store most vitamins, so in order to stay healthy, we need to eat fresh foods every day.

**China** A girl takes a polio vaccine at a UNICEF-assisted clinic. By vaccinating as many children as possible, the World Health Organization, UNICEF, and other partners hope to have freed the world from polio by 2005.

... The polio vaccine is quick and easy to take. The child just swallows the medicine! However, to be totally effective, you need to take it on four separate occasions.

# Natalie

Natalie suffers from eczema and from asthma, a condition affecting the tubes that carry air in and out of her lungs. There is no cure, but fortunately, Natalie is able to manage her condition and leads a very active life.

Eczema cream

### ECZEMA

Many asthmatics suffer from a skin condition called eczema. Natalie has to be careful what her skin comes into contact with. Some things make it break into sores.

. . . . "I have to moisturize my skin morning and evening. The hot weather makes my skin itchy. Once I start scratching, I cannot stop and my skin easily bleeds and gets infected."

SCOTLAND

IRELAND    UK

ENGLAND

WALES

FRANCE

## United Kingdom

Factories and traffic in developed countries, such as the UK, tend to create pollution. This can cause health problems such as asthma, which affects one in eight children in the UK.

### SPORTS

Exercise can trigger attacks for some asthma sufferers, but luckily that's not the case for Natalie. In fact, she finds that doing lots of sports has made her chest stronger, so she suffers from fewer colds and asthma attacks.

## TRIGGERS

Natalie can't have many stuffed animals, and she can't have pets or wear wool either because the dust from these can bring on an asthma attack. The family house has no carpets or curtains for the same reason.

## DIET

Natalie suffers from food allergies, so she must be careful about what she eats. Milk, cheese, and eggs could make her very sick.

Cheese

Egg

Milk

Spacer device

Reliever spray

Preventer spray

## INHALERS

Natalie treats her asthma with two inhaler sprays. She must use her preventer every day to calm her airways. Her reliever opens up her airways if she gets an attack.

"When I have an asthma attack, my chest feels all tight and horrible. Sometimes I cannot stop coughing. That's when I take my reliever to make it easier for me to breathe."

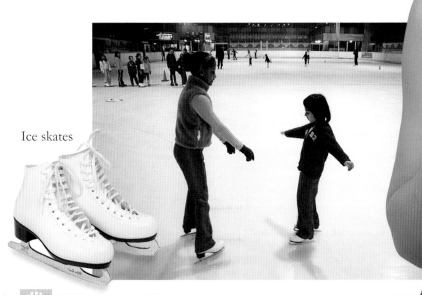

Ice skates

"I do gymnastics on Wednesday, swimming on Thursday, netball on Friday, and ice-skating on Saturday! I also like rollerblading and I do it whenever I can outside our house."

# 2. Development

**Education** is the right of every child. Education should help children to develop their personalities, talents, and abilities. It should also teach them to respect other people.

Development —noun; to develop —verb **1** to bring out the possibilities of. **2** to grow. **3** to mature or evolve.

Every child should have time and somewhere safe to **play.** All children should be allowed to have privacy if they want to spend some time on their own.

Every child has the right to an

# education

numeracy, literacy, stimulation,

# School rules!

## Human beings are always learning.

School gives you skills such as reading, writing, and math.
It also develops your personality, talents, and abilities.
Just as importantly, it teaches you your rights and
responsibilities, and guides you so you learn to respect others
and to live peacefully with them.

## skills, information, concepts

# Why do we need an education?

Do you ever wish you didn't have to go to school? Millions of children around the world can't ever go to school. More than half of them are girls.

• **If you can't read, write, or do simple math**, it is hard to find a good job, and people may take advantage of you. Without school, it is very difficult to escape poverty. Children who go to school get better jobs when they are older, they live longer, and are healthier.

• **School is more than reading, writing, and math.** School is a place to learn about self-respect and dignity, and to find out about our rights. School is also where we learn about staying healthy and how to prevent disease.

## Why are girls behind boys in literacy?

• One girl in four around the world who should be in school full time is not.

• In sub-Saharan Africa, about 40 percent of girls are not being educated.

• In some places, people do not believe that girls need an education.

• Some girls are kept at home to help around the house or to work on the family farm or business.

• Families that cannot afford to send all their children to school may only send the boys.

One out of every seven people around the world cannot read or write this sentence.

## Why isn't there education for everyone?

• **Some children live in places without schools or teachers.** In some places, there are no schools or not enough qualified teachers. Sometimes there are schools but they can't cater for children with disabilities or special needs.

• **Some can't afford school tuition.** Not all countries provide free education. Even when education is free, parents may not be able to afford the cost of books, school uniforms, and other equipment such as pens or notebooks.

• **Some work to help support their families.** Parents might only be able to afford an education for some of their children and may need the others to work and bring home wages. So in one family, some children may go to school and others may not.

• **Some have no families to help them.** Children who have run away from home or who are orphaned may be sleeping on city streets. They are struggling just to survive, and very few of them manage to get an education.

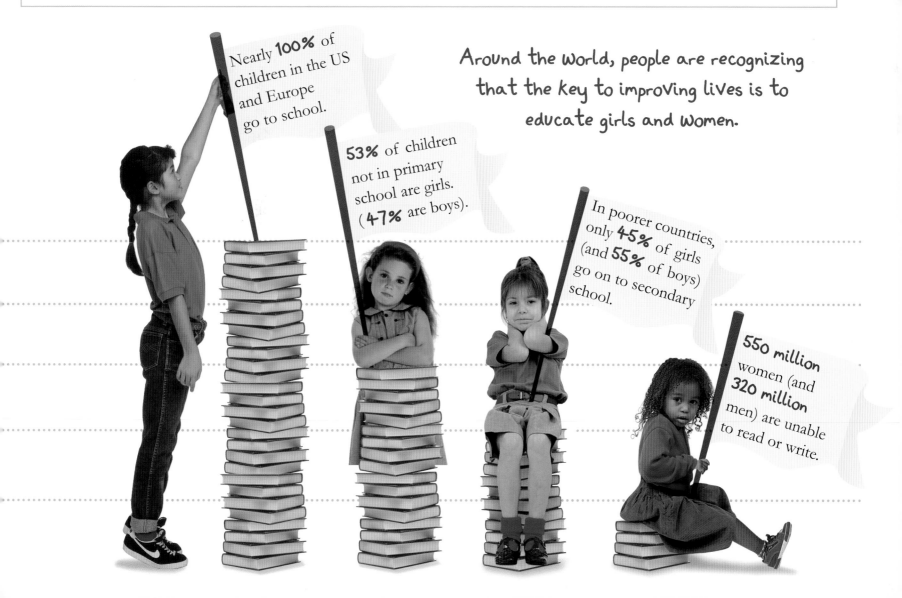

Nearly **100%** of children in the US and Europe go to school.

**53%** of children not in primary school are girls. (**47%** are boys).

Around the world, people are recognizing that the key to improving lives is to educate girls and women.

In poorer countries, only **45%** of girls (and **55%** of boys) go on to secondary school.

**550 million** women (and **320 million** men) are unable to read or write.

# School for all!

Education is the key to a better future for everyone, but for millions of children, going to school is no easy matter. All over the world, governments, nongovernmental organizations (NGOs), parents, and children themselves are finding ways to make sure that children receive the vital learning they need to improve their lives.

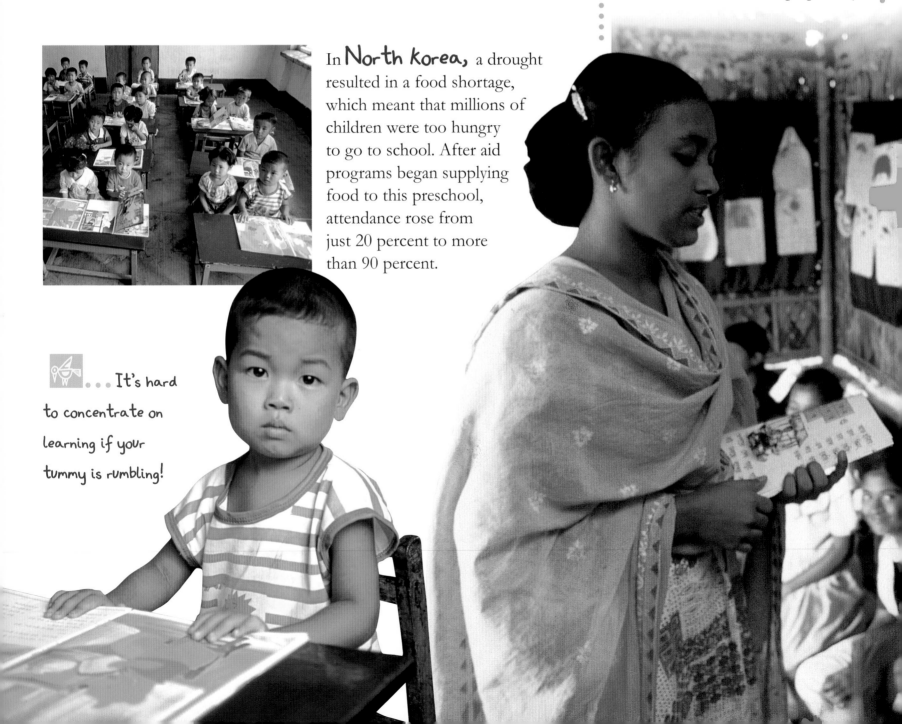

**Bangladesh** Until recently, this girl spent her days working in a clothing factory. Then the company she worked for agreed to stop hiring children and to help pay for them to go to school instead. Now she is learning how to read. Informal schools like this give former child workers a chance to escape poverty.

In **North korea,** a drought resulted in a food shortage, which meant that millions of children were too hungry to go to school. After aid programs began supplying food to this preschool, attendance rose from just 20 percent to more than 90 percent.

✂ . . . It's hard to concentrate on learning if your tummy is rumbling!

... This girl was lucky. Some children have to work, and so miss out on going to school. Schools need to offer these children part-time schooling so they don't miss out completely.

... Education is so important that when a child cannot go to school, the school must come to the child.

Some **Australian** children living in the outback are hundreds of miles from the nearest school. The only way they can study is by talking to their teachers on two-way radios and sending in their homework by mail.

**Kenya** For thousands of orphaned children, like 12-year-old Thomas, getting an education was just a dream until he started attending a UNICEF-assisted center in Nairobi. The center provides education, counseling, and skills training to children who are living or working on the streets. For these children, it's much more than just a school — it's a lifeline.

School gives you hope.

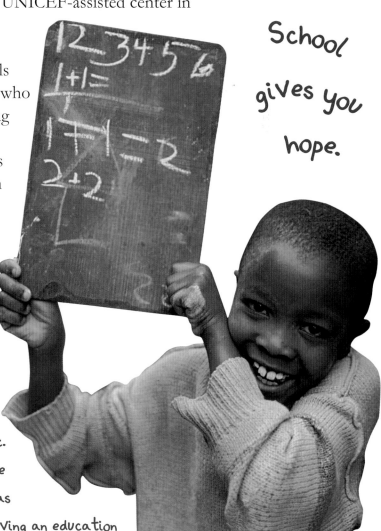

... Thomas displays his new skills in arithmetic. He has lived on the streets since he was 10 years old. Receiving an education means he has a brighter future.

# Sbongile

## UNIFORM

Sbongile wears a white shirt and a navy blue and white sweatsuit to school. It has the school emblem on it and says "Ellerton."

Just a few years ago, Sbongile could not have attended Ellerton Primary School in South Africa. At that time, the apartheid laws prevented black and white people from mixing. Those laws have now been completely abolished.

### EARLY BIRD

Ellerton is near the beach in Sea Point, a long way from Sbongile's home. Sbongile's mother wakes her up at 4:30 a.m. so she can be picked up for the trip to school at 5:50 a.m.

.... "A driver picks up 16 of us from our houses. I am the first one he picks up and then he picks up the other children. I get to school at 7:30 a.m."

.... "I take books, pencils, and a reading book to school. Sometimes I take sandwiches, tuna, and polony (processed meat) or cheese and bacon and egg salad. Sometimes my mother gives me money to buy a pie or a samosa from the cafeteria."

BOTSWANA

NAMIBIA

LESOTHO

SOUTH AFRICA

## South Africa

At the southern tip of the African continent lies South Africa. The country is rich in natural resources including coal, tin, iron ore, gold, and diamonds.

## LANGUAGES

Pupils at Ellerton speak at least seven languages other than English and Afrikaans. These include the African languages of Xhosa, Zulu, and Sotho.

"There are 23 children in my class. We are lucky, because in some of the other classes, there are about 40. We sit in groups of six."

## MURALS

The school is decorated with bright murals. Sbongile loves Ellerton, but when she first started she felt the rules were very strict.

" In the playground we play four blocks and cops and robbers. But my favorites are games with a tennis ball, which I play with my friends."

Sbongile's math book

## ASSEMBLY

There is an assembly once a week where the children sing their school song and the national anthem. Lessons include math, English, Afrikaans, science, and history. Sbongile's favorite is science because there is so much to learn.

"Sometimes in our class we bake and make snacks. In music, we sing songs. We also do computers, art, and library lessons. In the summer, we swim in the school's swimming pool."

Sbongile's picture

Sbongile and her friends

# Maria

For six years, girls in Afghanistan were not allowed to go to school at all. Now, things have changed. Maria attends a girls' school in Kabul run by the new government with help from UNICEF.

## LIFE IN AFGHANISTAN

In 2002, a new government came to power in Afghanistan. Since then, there have been schools and educational opportunities for women. Maria was lucky that there were schools she could go to by the time she reached school age.

 "During the time I was too young to go to school I studied at home. My older sister Tamana helped me learn how to read and write."

## Afghanistan

Fewer than one in five women (and one in two men) can read in Afghanistan. Now, under a new government, much more schooling is available for girls.

## AN EARLY START

Maria has to get up early so she can be at school by 7 a.m. She wears the school uniform, a nice black tunic and pants with a white headscarf.

"It takes 30 minutes to walk to school from our house. I go to school with two of my sisters. My brothers go to a different school."

## TIME FOR LEARNING

The girls sit on a rug during classes. Maria sits next to her best friend, Hafiza. She studies hard because she would like to become a teacher.

...."My favorite subject is Dari (Afghan Persian), which is the language that we speak. I find it easy."

## FUN WITH FRIENDS

Maria plays with her friends and also eats a snack she has brought from home. Maria's school is only for girls.

...."I like to jump rope during recess, but my favorite thing about school is playing soccer!"

## A GIFT FROM UNICEF

Every child at Maria's school received a special school bag and notebooks from UNICEF.

School bag

School books

...."Two of my wishes are to have a new house and to stay in Kabul."

ما / کی

Maria's name in Dari

"I want to be a teacher."

# Every child has the right to

# play

## running, jumping, skipping,

# A serious business

Playing is actually very important.
You don't need expensive toys, just a good imagination.
Kids don't need to speak the same language to play together.
Sports exercise your body, team games teach you to work
with other people, and play that involves pretending
lets you use your imagination.

## pretending, imagining, laughing

# What's the point of playing?

**Play** might not seem like an essential activity, but it is. Playing is the main way children prepare for growing up.

- **Playing on your own** teaches you to think for yourself and to enjoy your own company.
- **Playing with others** teaches you to get along with other people and work well in a group.
- **Playing allows you** to be creative and enables you to explore the world around you safely.
- **Playing trains you** to be resourceful and to use your imagination.

## pretending, acting, singing,

**Many children** don't get the chance to play.

- You have to **work** long hours.

- It is too **polluted, dirty, or unsafe** outside.

- **There is a war,** or a war has recently ended.

- You have **suffered** mentally or emotionally.

# How many different ways to play can you think of?

- **You can play by yourself** by jumping on your bed, reading a book, dressing up, or keeping a diary.

- **You can make things** by drawing or painting, building a model airplane, baking a cake, or making a monster.

- **You can take part in sports.** Team sports like football or soccer teach you how to get along with others. Gymnastics, running, and swimming teach you to rely on yourself. All sports help keep you fit and healthy.

- **You can have a hobby** like collecting stickers or rocks, playing an instrument, doing magic tricks, or taking care of a pet.

- **You can play with others** in the playground, in the park, using board games, or by inventing your own games.

You don't need toys to play, but you do need time and a place to be by yourself or with your friends.

**Adults keep out!**

It's hard to play with adults looking over your shoulder.

All children are entitled to their privacy.

building, hiding, seeking, chasing, painting

## That's because it's hard to play when:

- You have **no energy** because you don't get enough food to eat.

- There is **not enough room** to play inside your house.

- You have to **take care of** your younger brothers and sisters all the time.

- You are physically **sick.**

Playing can be messy!

# Just playing

Children are the experts when it comes to playing! Indoors or outdoors, whether or not there are toys to play with, kids can always find a way to keep busy and have fun.

**South Africa** Children are playing in a daycare in King William's Town.

**Botswana** Playing a game called *Makaroo*, a boy sits in the middle of a circle of chairs while other boys run around him.

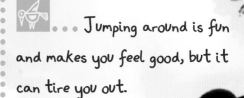 . . . There are games that you can only play when there are lots of people to have fun with. What other games can you think of that require a lot of players?

. . . Jumping around is fun and makes you feel good, but it can tire you out.

**Philippines** Building blocks and jigsaw puzzles demand quietness and concentration. It's easy to become very absorbed in this kind of play.

... Sometimes it's nice to play close to other people without actually playing with them. You can share ideas but still do things your own way.

**Peru** Look at how this boy is using his whole body. Soccer involves all of you, not just your feet and a ball!

... Soccer is probably the most popular game in the world.

**Kenya** This Somali boy holds a toy bus he created out of paper and cardboard. It took a lot of time and imagination to make this toy.

... You can play by making something, and then you can play with the thing you've made!

**Cuba** Three Ukrainian boys play chess at a camp providing medical assistance to children who have suffered exposure to radiation.

... A game of chess can take hours because the players spend so much time thinking carefully about the moves they will make.

# Michael

A sheep and cattle station in the South Australian outback is home to Michael, his sister, and their parents. Because he lives so far from a school, Michael does his schoolwork alone and talks to his teacher over a two-way radio.

## AUSTRALIA

### Australia

Australia's population is small in relation to its size. Some farming families live hundreds of miles from their neighbors.

## ANIMALS

In addition to cattle and sheep, there are other animals at the station. The family keep *chooks* (chickens) for their eggs and ducks for their meat. There are dogs and also horses used for *mustering* (rounding up) the cattle.

. . . "I help feed and water the dogs, chooks, ducks, horses, and cattle. When I grow up, I would like my own cattle station so I could be like Dad."

## OUTDOORS

Michael spends a lot of time outdoors. He loves taking the dogs for a run and riding his bike around the station. Twice a year, he goes to camp where he meets other children his age.

## SHEEP

There are 1,200 sheep and 550 cattle on the ranch. Once a year, the sheep are sheared for their wool. Even Michael and Rebecca get involved, although most of the work is done by hired sheep hands.

... "I talk to my friend, Naish, on the school radio after my lessons. He lives on Bulgunnia Station, 390 miles (630 km) from here."

## AUSSIE RULES

The ball is kicked in Aussie Rules soccer, but players are also allowed to catch and run with it. Michael and Rebecca practice, but they can't play a real game – you need two teams of 18 players for that!

Michael's favorite book

... "The best things about living in the outback are the windmills, the open spaces, and sunsets. The worst thing is not being able to see my friends."

Michael's favorite teddy bear

## TOYS AND GAMES

Michael plays on his own with his toys – trucks, tractors, and a motorcycle. He loves reading *Outback Magazine,* and he also watches television and plays games on his computer.

# 3. Protection

Every child should have someone to **love and care** for them.

Every child should be protected from **work** that could harm or exploit them.

Protection – noun; to protect – verb **1** to defend or guard from attack, invasion, loss, insult, etc.; cover; shield from harm.

# Disability should not prevent any child from participating fully in life.

Children need protection from the fighting and destruction of **War**.

Every child needs

# love and care

love, care, hugs, support,

# Someone to take care of you

Children need the support of caring adults.
It's often parents who have this job, but not always.
Adult carers should do whatever is best for the child.
Every child needs an adult who can listen to them,
comfort them when they are hurt or sad,
and encourage them to be sensitive to others.

safety, laughter, company

# Who loves and cares for you?

**Everyone** needs someone to take care of them.

• **You don't just share** a home with the people you live with – you also share your life with them. They love you and take care of you.

• **Children can live** with mothers, fathers, aunts, uncles, cousins, bigger brothers or sisters, grandparents, stepparents, foster parents, adoptive parents, parents' girlfriends or boyfriends, or just friends.

• **Your family** can have just one other person, or 20. They can be young or old, male or female – the important thing is that they care for you.

## Love makes the world go round.

They cook your **dinner** and make you eat all your **vegetables**.

They ask if you have any **homework** to do and try to **help** you do it.

Before you could read, they told you **bedtime stories** and **sang** to you.

Mothers, grandmothers, aunts, cousins, stepmothers, foster mothers, adoptive mothers, carers

Big brothers let you play with them.

Little brothers give you hugs and kisses.

# Some families can't take care of their children because of...

• **Poverty** Some families are overwhelmed by poverty and just can't afford to care for all of their children. In such a situation, a child might have to leave home to find work.

• **Death** When parents die, children often go to live with relatives. If no one can take care of orphaned children, they may end up homeless.

• **War** In the 1990s, more than 1 million children were orphaned or separated from their families by war. Organizations such as UNICEF help reunite them.

• **Violence** in the home is an awful reality for some. Child victims of violence may run away and end up living on the streets.

## What then?

The government makes sure that these children are taken care of by providing orphanages or foster homes for them, or by finding adoptive parents.

### Growing up alone

More than 13 million children under 15 have lost one or both parents to AIDS.

At least 1 million children a year are left motherless by death in childbirth.

Millions of children live on their own on the streets of the world's cities.

## Think of what your family does for you.

They usually buy you the **clothes** and **shoes** you wear.

They make you **clean up** your room and tell you when to **go to bed!**

They try to **help** you in every way they can.

Fathers, grandfathers, uncles, cousins, stepfathers, foster fathers, adoptive fathers, carers

Big sisters let you play with them.

Little sisters give you hugs and kisses.

# Family feelings

Just like people, families come in different shapes and sizes. Family members are often related to one another, but they don't have to be. It also doesn't matter how many there are in your family, as long as you all support and love each other.

**Burundi** Terrible fighting has raged in Burundi, leaving many orphans. A woman called Maggy opened a foster home where she takes care of all the children in the photograph below.

... Children who are temporarily without a home may live in foster care. Eventually, they might return home or be adopted permanently by a new family.

**Lesotho** This mother and her son live in a center run by Catholic nuns. There are more than 40 young women living there, some of whom have children of their own. The women learn skills and produce goods that are sold at the local market.

... Some parents no longer live together. Their children normally live with either their mother or their father, but typically they may visit their other parent.

**England** This family consists of a mother, a father, and a child whom they have adopted. Children whose parents are dead or unable to care for them may be permanently adopted by a new family. People who want to adopt children have to be checked out to make sure they will be good parents.

... It's all right for adopted children to think about their biological parents sometimes, even if they are happy and secure with their adoptive family.

**Pakistan** Families where several generations live together are common in many countries. In Pakistan, when a man gets married, his bride usually joins him in his parents' home. Their children grow up surrounded by aunts, uncles, and cousins.

... In a large family like this, you never need a babysitter because there is always someone around to help take care of the children!

**China** This is a small family. It consists of two parents and just one child.

... China is slightly smaller than the US, but it contains more than four times as many people. It is a very densely populated country.

**Finland** There are 20 children in the Oikarinen family – 6 sons and 14 daughters. Their ages range from 3 to 27 years old.

... The average number of children in a Finnish family is just 1.8, but Bertta and Seppo Oikarinen belong to a religious movement that encourages people to have large families.

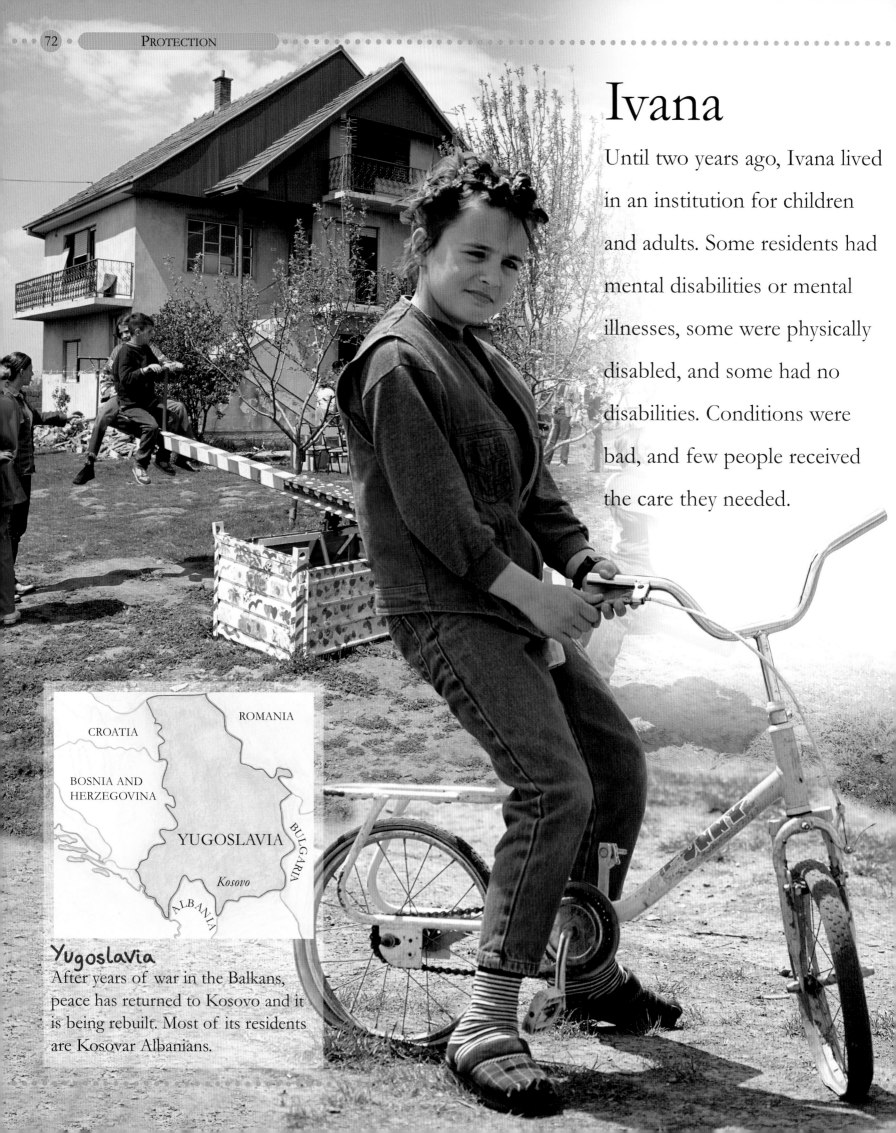

# Ivana

Until two years ago, Ivana lived in an institution for children and adults. Some residents had mental disabilities or mental illnesses, some were physically disabled, and some had no disabilities. Conditions were bad, and few people received the care they needed.

## Yugoslavia

After years of war in the Balkans, peace has returned to Kosovo and it is being rebuilt. Most of its residents are Kosovar Albanians.

### CHILDREN'S HOME

When she was 10, Ivana came to live in a brand-new children's home with just eight other children and caring staff.

... "I stay up late to talk and to play with my toys together with Marina and Jasmina, my roommates. They are my best friends. I am very happy in my new home."

### CARERS

The staff at the home care for the children like parents and give them lots of love and hugs.

... "One day I want to be a nurse and give babies injections really slowly so it does not hurt them and they don't cry."

### SCHOOL

Ivana received no education in the institution. Since coming to live in the home, she has started attending the local primary school.

... "I like school, but not when there is too much homework and I don't have time to play with my friends in the home."

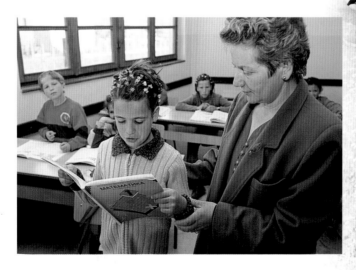

"All my toys are good!"

No child should be exploited through

# Work

tiring, low wages, long hours,

# Working for a living

Most adults have to work to earn money.
Many children have to work to help their family.
When children work, they don't have time for other things.
Work can be a fun and important part of growing up, but no
work should be harmful or take the place of learning, playing,
and having time to enjoy being a child.

boring, no free time, exploitation

# Why do children work?

More than **210 million** children between ages five and 14 work for a living. More than half of them work in dangerous jobs. Children often work long hours for little pay in poor conditions.

• Most children who work full time do it to help their families. Even when children are not well paid, their income can make a big difference.

• Child workers are deprived of the simple joys of childhood and are forced into a life of drudgery.

• Many businesses employ young children because they can be paid very little or nothing at all and can be easily taken advantage of.

• Some work is dangerous and can lead to stunted growth and accidents.

• Some part-time work is all right for children.

• It is important to know the difference between child labor that takes advantage of children, and work that does them no harm.

## Not all work is bad for children.

**Some types of work can be all right if –**
- You are not too young for the job.
- You can stop any time you want to.
- It does not interfere with school or play.
- You are paid decent wages.
- It is not dangerous to your physical or mental health.
- You have time to spend with your family.
- You are treated fairly and have someone to complain to if you are not.

**Working is wrong when –**
- You are too young for the job.
- It involves unsafe or harmful work or working conditions.
- You cannot stop when you want to.
- There is little or no pay.
- It prevents you from going to school or takes the place of school.
- It separates you from your family.
- You are treated unfairly or abused.

**Problems with child labor**

Some types of labor are not acceptable for children and should not be tolerated anywhere.

## Many children never get the chance to just be children.

- **73 million working children** are under 10. In the short term, they miss out on education, and in the long term, they are more likely to die early.

- In Brazil, Kenya, and Mexico, at least one in four farm workers is **under 15 years old.**

- Sometimes children **as young as eight** are taken to other countries to work.

- Children often work the **longest hours** and are the **worst treated** of all laborers.

- Millions of girls work long hours as **domestic laborers** in private homes where beatings and harassment are common.

- In sub-Saharan Africa, **23 percent of all children** between the ages of 5 and 14 work.

# Hard work

Most countries have laws that limit the hours children are allowed to work and control the age at which they can work full-time. The major reason for these laws is that children already have work to do – schoolwork – and that is what should come first.

**Ecuador** Rosita, like one-third of Ecuador's population, works in agriculture. Here, she helps harvest wheat. It is extremely hard work if done by hand and not by machine.

Agricultural work is often seasonal. At harvest time, schools in farming areas may close down so that children can help their families to gather in the crops.

**Mauritania** Mame Diara is an orphan living with her cousins. She does most of the household chores, including cleaning, cooking, and taking care of the family's animals.

When we think about child labor, we often forget that millions of children are working not in fields or factories but in private homes.

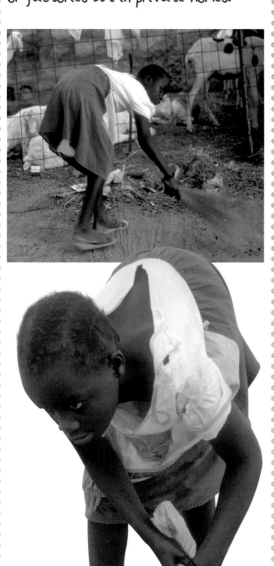

**England** Douglas lives on his dad's farm. He helps out whenever he is not at school. His main job is feeding the family's three sheepdogs and two pet dogs.

The kind of work that Douglas does is not exploitative. British children are allowed to work a few hours a day, as long as the work does not harm them and their education is not affected.

**Iraq** Ten-year-old Dana sells candy on a street in Erbil. Dana does not earn very much money for the long hours he works. He also runs the risk of getting sick or of being robbed.

In addition to missing out on their education, child workers on the streets are also easy targets for criminals. These children are vulnerable to violence and abuse.

# Arif

A special program has given Arif, who lives in a slum, the chance to work as a reporter on a television show for, by, and about children. The show, *Mukta Khabor*, has allowed Arif to excel.

## Bangladesh

Sixty percent of people in Bangladesh do not have enough money to live on. Almost 25 percent of the population are between 12 and 17 years old.

RICKSHAW WORKSHOP
Like many other slum children, Arif had a job as well as attending school. It was hard work and very badly paid.

... "My hands used to really ache after days of work painting rickshaws. Now things are very different."

Bicycle rickshaw

## CHILD REPORTER

The young crew of *Mukta Khabor* research, report, and run the newsroom entirely on their own. They have become role models for other young Bangladeshis.

*Mukta Khabor* logo

## PAINTING

Arif discovered he had a talent for art and became a good painter through his job at the rickshaw workshop. He still enjoys painting in his free time.

... "I like it when local people tell my parents they saw me on television."

... "I earn four times more than in my old job, and I learn new things every day."

## FAMILY

Arif has three brothers – Sharif is nine, Rajiv is seven, and Raju is four. Arif is happy that he can help his family with the money he earns from *Mukta Khabor*.

Arif's art

... "If I were president, I would help parents so they don't have to send their children to work."

## COMMUNAL KITCHEN

Arif's mother prepares a meal of fish in the kitchen the family shares with other families. Everyone in the family eats together.

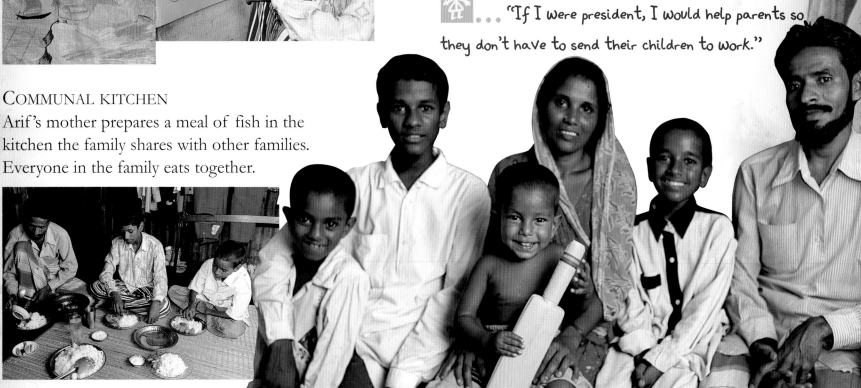

# No child should fight in a

# War

## danger, confusion, fear,

# Not for kids

War is a fact of life for many children.

War uproots families and destroys communities.

After a war, children need help rebuilding their lives.

Children are the most innocent victims of war. They are sometimes even dragged into wars and forced to fight against their will. These children are robbed of their childhood.

machines, soldiers, destruction

# What happens in a war?

**No child** ever started a war, but children fight and die in wars **every day**.

No child should have to live through a war.

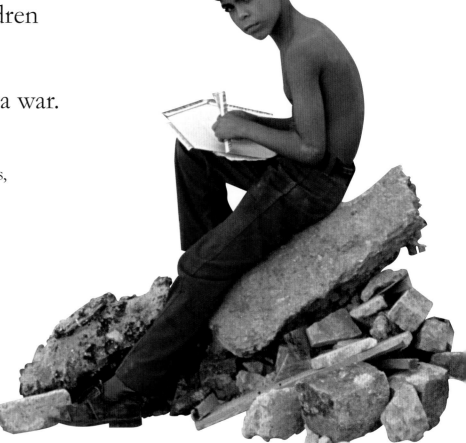

- **Normal life** is impossible during war. Communities break down when people are forced to leave their homes, and schools and hospitals are destroyed.

- **Families** are damaged by war. Children may become separated from their families. Many people are killed or injured, both physically and emotionally.

- **The damage** continues long after the war is over. Children and their families must somehow put their lives back together and learn how to live normally again.

## War is not a **game.**

During the 1990s, more than **2 million children** died in wars.

**28 million women and children** had to flee.

Armed conflicts are raging in more than **30 countries**.

**6 million children** have wounds from war.

## Children have the right to be protected from the dangers of war.

War kills, but it also destroys normal life
in many other ways.

• **War destroys life.** Most of the people who die or are injured in war are not soldiers but ordinary people who cannot fight back. It is women, children, and elderly people who suffer the most.

• **War destroys childhood.** Children who have seen horrible things respond in different ways. Some may feel depressed or hopeless about the future. Others might become angry or violent.

• **War destroys homes.** During war, people are forced to leave their homes and their countries and become refugees. Often, they never come back. Wars have made millions of children homeless.

• **War destroys play.** Long after a war is over, landmines buried in schools, playgrounds, and fields continue to wound or kill children and adults.

PERIGO MINAS!

DANGER MINES

### Facts about landmines

Each year, more than 10,000 children are killed or hurt by landmines.

Children are at risk from landmines in 90 countries.

A landmine can cost less than $3 to manufacture – and $1,000 to find and dispose of safely.

# In war, innocent people suffer.

Millions more died from hunger and disease caused by war.

Many of them never return to their homes.

Around 300,000 children are fighting in wars.

Landmines kill or injure nearly 30 children every day.

Children affected by war may need help recovering.

# War and recovery

War is bad for everyone, but particularly for innocent children. How do wars and conflicts affect children? And how are children helped to recover after the fighting ends?

Hands linked, these former child soldiers board a UN airplane that will take them to a better life.

**Sudan** During the civil war, these children were forced to become soldiers. Now they are being flown to transit centers where they will receive health care, education, and counseling to help them recover from their experiences. UNICEF and other organizations will make every effort to trace their families. It is hoped that they will soon be able to return home and resume a normal life.

**Leaving war behind** The real work begins after the fighting has stopped. Homes and communities are rebuilt and families reunited. Schools reopen and children begin to catch up on what they have missed.

**Recovery kit** A kit containing high-protein bars, bandages, school supplies, and a T-shirt saying "All Children. All Rights. Everywhere" is given to former Sudanese child soldiers to help them get back to normal.

**Rwanda** These boys from Rwanda have survived the fighting. Now they are receiving support to help them deal with their wartime experiences. Here, in a trauma treatment center run with UNICEF support, they wield fake guns that they have made themselves and act out some of the things they have witnessed.

... This family was separated during war but has been reunited with help from aid agencies.

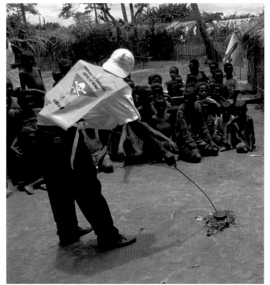

**Angola** Although the war is now over, danger still lurks just beneath the surface. This man teaches children in a displaced persons' camp to beware of buried landmines. It is estimated that there are still between 10 and 15 million unexploded landmines in Angola, and as many as 50–100 million unexploded landmines scattered in countries throughout the world.

Deactivated landmines

... Landmines are very cruel weapons. Most injuries are suffered by civilians long after the conflict is over.

**Yugoslavia** A child refugee from Kosovo holds an umbrella over his mother, who is cradling her younger child in her arms. The family is waiting to board a bus that will take them to safety in neighboring Albania. Having left home in a hurry, these refugees, like many others, have abandoned their homes and most of their possessions.

... Families frequently become separated in the rush to escape a conflict. UNICEF works to reunite these children and their parents.

*Names have been changed to protect the people involved.*

"I like soccer. If I don't become a doctor, I might want to become a professional soccer player."

# Isa

During the war in Sierra Leone, some fighters came to Isa's house and took him away. After two years, he was released, along with other children caught up in the war. He is now back home.

## BACK TOGETHER AGAIN

An organization called Caritas took care of Isa for a year. Then he went back to his family. Isa recently went to a Christmas party organized by Caritas.

"I have two brothers called T-Boy and Yasuf and two sisters called Sally and Kai. My new baby sister, Marie, is just five months old. I also play with my cousins, who are called Momoh, Jeneba, and Fatu."

## Sierra Leone

Raging civil war in Sierra Leone resulted in many deaths. Almost one in three people fled from their homes.

GUINEA

SIERRA LEONE

LIBERIA

## PLAYING WITH FRIENDS

Isa has no toys of his own, but there are always children around to play with.

*...* "I like playing checkers with my best friend, Brima. Another game we play is called balancing ball."

Playing balancing ball

## HARVEST TIME

Nobody plants crops during a war because they might have to leave before the food can be harvested. Now that there is peace, Isa has planted some groundnuts.

*...* "I would like to help my country because a lot has been destroyed and needs rebuilding."

*"I want to be a doctor."*

## TIME FOR SCHOOL

Wearing his school uniform and reading a book, Isa walks with his father. At school, Isa studies math, English, geography, social studies, and the Bible.

*...* "I lost three years of school because of the fighting. I am now 10 years old, and I am really happy at the school I go to. My favorite subject is English."

# No child should be held back by a

# disability

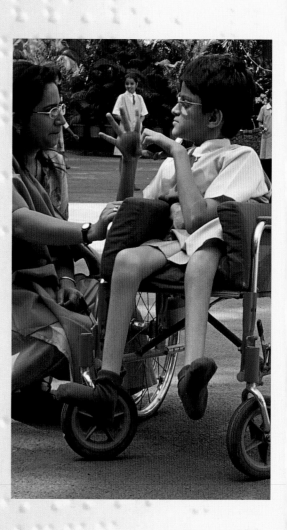

respect, opportunity, patience,

# Enjoying a good life

We all deserve the chance to do our best.
Disabled people may need some extra help.
Help starts with understanding and caring.
We can't always prevent people from being disabled, but
we can make sure that disabled people have the same
opportunities as everyone else.

encouragement, understanding

# What is life like with a disability?

**Imagine** trying to move around if your legs didn't work or communicating if you couldn't hear or see clearly.

- **Children** who are disabled are just like everyone else except that some parts of their bodies do not work very well. Disabled children can lead normal, full, wonderful lives as long as they receive the right kind of support.

- The biggest **problem** that disabled children face is when people do not understand their needs. Letting disabled children speak, and listening to what they have to say, are the best ways to help them.

## Disability can have some effect on your life.

- Sometimes disabled children need *equipment.*

- *Training* and *education* can help disabled people.

- *Operations* and *medicine* can help some disabilities.

- Disabled people want to be *treated normally.*

A disability can be many things. It can be –

- **Physical** – a difficulty with part of the body.

- **Mental** – some disabilities make it hard to think.

- **Visible** – such as a missing limb, or the inability to walk.

- **Invisible** – such as deafness or dyslexia.

Disability can happen in many ways.

- Some children are **born** disabled. Some children are disabled in **accidents**.

- Some children are disabled by **war**. Some children are disabled by **disease**.

**Children** with **disabilities** should not be discriminated against. They should be given equal treatment, education, jobs, and a chance to lead **normal lives**.

Or it can affect your life a lot.

They may use **hearing aids** or **artificial limbs**.

Blind people can learn to use a **guide dog**.

An **operation** may help repair a damaged limb.

# Living with a disability

Having a disability does not neccessarily mean you can't see, speak, hear, or walk; it may just take a little more effort to do things. Doctors can sometimes help to ease a disability, but most disabled people cope by being resourceful and finding alternative ways of doing things. Like everyone else, they appreciate people behaving considerately toward them.

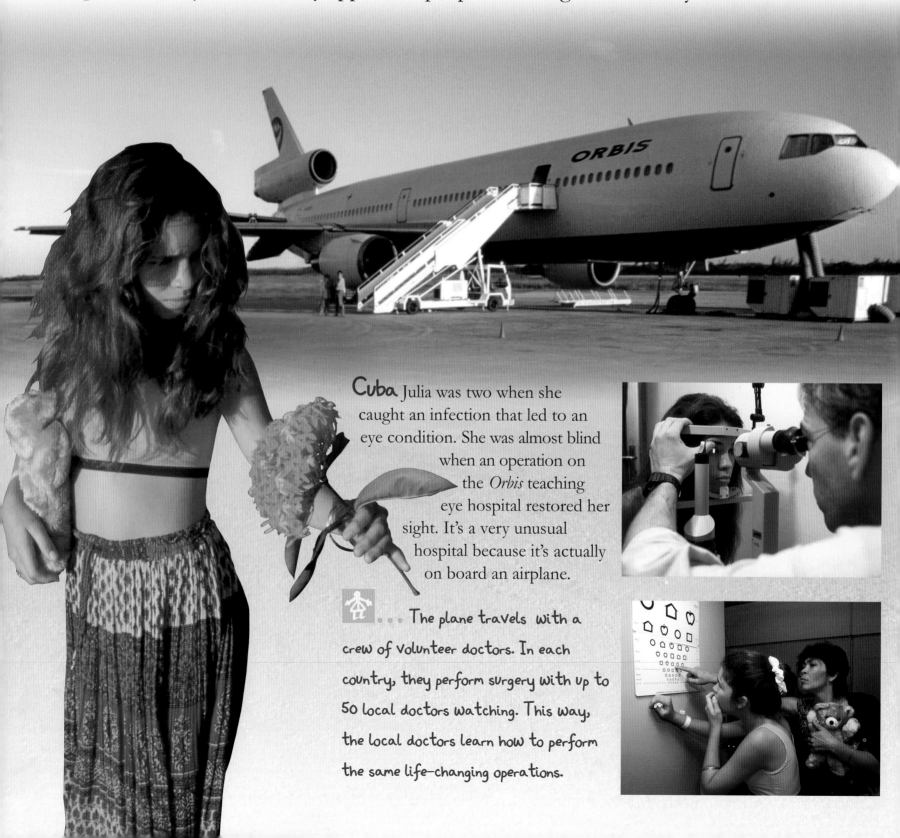

**Cuba** Julia was two when she caught an infection that led to an eye condition. She was almost blind when an operation on the *Orbis* teaching eye hospital restored her sight. It's a very unusual hospital because it's actually on board an airplane.

. . . The plane travels with a crew of volunteer doctors. In each country, they perform surgery with up to 50 local doctors watching. This way, the local doctors learn how to perform the same life-changing operations.

**Jamaica** This little girl cannot walk, but that doesn't mean she needs help to move around. The metal rails on the back of her wheelchair allow her to be mobile by using her arms.

... When there is a problem with one part of the body, another part may be able to take over its job.

**Romania** Using a mirror, a speech therapist at a kindergarten helps a child practice speaking. There are many different reasons why people might find it difficult to speak. They might be hard of hearing, or have difficulty controlling the muscles that are responsible for speech, or maybe the part of their brain that deals with speech has been damaged.

... With help and encouragement, children who find it difficult to speak clearly, or to talk at all, can improve their language skills and speak more confidently.

**Nicaragua** Deaf people may learn to use sign language to communicate with each other. Sign language differs from country to country.

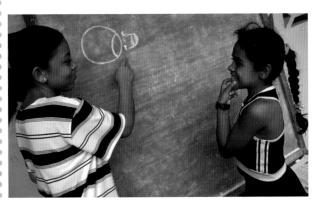

... Deaf people may also learn to read lips. By watching the mouth of the person speaking, they can figure out what words are being said.

**Yugoslavia** Burim from Kosovo lost his legs in an accident, but he is learning to walk again using artificial legs and a walker. Eventually, he hopes to be able to walk on his new legs unaided.

... Physically disabled people can participate and excel in sports. The very best disabled athletes compete in the world-class Paralympic Games.

# C.J.

When he was five, C.J. – of Atlanta,
Georgia – was hit by a car. He
had to re-learn how to walk,
talk, and even eat. These days,
despite some mental
disabilities, C.J. is an
avid soccer player.

## FAMILY SUPPORT
C.J.'s family is proud of his athletic skills.
They always come to support him when
he plays a soccer game.

... "C.J. has overcome a lot to get where
he is today. He doesn't let anything deter him.
He is a blessed child." – C.J.'s mother

## US
The United States is the
third largest country in the
world in both its physical
size and population.

## RECOVERY
CJ's parents were
told he wouldn't be
able to recognize
them when he woke
from his coma, but
he knew who they
were right away.

**Therapy:** Focus on patients and families

### Back from the brink

Love gives a helping hand

## SPECIAL OLYMPICS

C.J. plays soccer with the Special Olympics. It runs sports events worldwide for people with mental disabilities.

... "Our soccer team is called the Trickum Tigers. I like being the defender, and I like getting a chance to kick the ball."

## SOCCER FANS

Although it is not as popular as some other sports, many people in the US play soccer. In 1994, the country even hosted the World Cup.

... "There are eight kids on my team. We practice every morning. We play against other kids in tournaments."

C.J.'s soccer shoes

## FUTURE

C.J. has recovered well from his accident, but he still goes to physical therapy at the local hospital and has speech therapy lessons at school.

... "I want to be a fireman so I can help people when there is a fire in their house."

## SPORTS TROPHIES

As well as soccer, C.J. has received trophies in recent years for playing baseball, basketball, and bowling.

# 4. Participation

Every child has the right to an **identity**, including a name, nationality, and religion.

Participation – noun; to participate – verb 1 to take part or to share with others. 2 to form a partnership with others. 3 to share benefits.

Every child has the right to freedom of **expression**.

A good **life**, lived to its full potential,

is the right of every child.

# Every child has the right to an

# identity

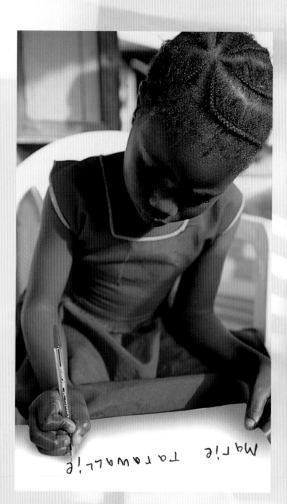

## name, nationality, religion,

# Who am I?

Everyone needs to belong to a community.
Some children are excluded from a community because they do not have a name or a nationality.
When you have a name, a nationality, and the right to practice your religion, you can fully participate in the life of your country and community.

## family, culture, community

# Who are you?

**What** is your name? Where are you from? What religion do you practice? No one should be able to take your identity from you.

## Your **name** is special.
## What does it mean to you?

• **Your name** might mean something in the language you speak or in a language that is part of your religion or culture.

• **Your name** may have been chosen for you by someone in your family or by a leader of your community.

• **Your name** connects you to members of your family and your community, both to those living and those who have died.

• **Your name** is a part of you. People should respect you by making the effort to call you by your correct name.

## People should be free to

**There are many** different religions — such as Christianity, Islam, Judaism, Hinduism, and Buddhism.

**Each religion** has its own teachings — Jews have the Torah. Hindus have the Vedas. Muslims have the Koran.

**Every religion** has different holidays — Muslims celebrate Eid ul-Fitr. Buddhists celebrate Wesak Day.

**Each religion** has its own holy places — Buddhists have Lhasa. Sikhs have Amritsar. Muslims have Mecca.

**Each religion** has different forms of worship — some use silence, some use spoken prayers or chanting.

Everyone is born somewhere, so why doesn't everyone have a **nationality**?

- **Sometimes children** do not get registered when they are born because their parents are afraid of going to the government offices.

- **Sometimes governments** take away the nationality of certain people in their country. Often this is caused by war, and often it causes war.

- **Sometimes children** become refugees because of war. When this happens, they may have to live in another country where they do not have any nationality.

- **Sometimes governments** deny nationality to people who belong to a particular ethnic group.

## What can governments do?

Find all the children who are not registered and grant them nationality. Recognize everyone born in that country as a citizen. Help all refugees to return home.

# practice all religions.

Other religions include Sikhism, Rastafarianism, Zoroastrianism, Bahai, Jainism, and many others besides.

Christians have the Bible. Sikhs have the Guru Granth Sahib. Buddhists have the Thripitaka.

Hindus celebrate Diwali. Christians celebrate Christmas. Sikhs celebrate Baisakhi. Jews celebrate Passover.

Christians, Jews, and Muslims have Jerusalem. Hindus have Varanasi. Roman Catholic Christians have Rome.

Some religions use singing or dancing, some use meditation, some use special foods, some light candles.

# What's in a name?

Your name is an important part of your identity. It is part of who you are, and it is one way that other people know you. Can you imagine what your life would be like if you did not have a name? Children's names are special to them and to their parents.

What does your name mean?

"Bilal is a gentle name and it was the name of the first person who said the call to prayer."

**Jasleen** and **Ravina** are friends. Their names are from the Punjabi language. Jasleen means "divine princess." Ravina means a "strong, free spirit."

**Bilal's** parents wanted a name that would reflect his Muslim religion, so they named him Bilal, after a companion of the prophet Mohammed.

"My parents chose the name Ravina for me because they expected me to be strong, with a free spirit and character. My parents also named me after a famous river called the River Ravi."

**Paul** The name Paul originally meant "little." It is also the name of one of the 12 apostles of Jesus Christ.

"My name doesn't mean anything special to my parents. They just liked the sound of it."

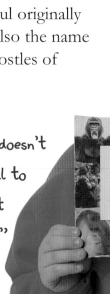

**Junique** In Junique's family, her name means "very special."

. . . . "My dad thought I was unique, so he put a 'J' in front of 'unique' to make Junique. Both my parents agreed on my name."

. . . . "My parents liked the sound of the name Mark, so that's what they called me."

**Mark** was a very important person in the Bible. He was one of the 12 apostles of Jesus.

**Meena** means "princess." Her parents named her Meena because she was special, just like a princess.

. . . . "I like my name. It makes me feel special."

**Meegan** is an old English word that means "strong." Meegan's middle name is Timothea, which means "honoring God."

. . . . "I like my name. My parents want me to live up to the meaning of my name."

**Teresa** In Chinese, the name Teresa sounds the same as the word for "happy."

. . . . "My mother named me Teresa because she was very happy when I was born."

**Haresh** is a Hindi name. The first part of Haresh's name, "Har," means God.

. . . . "When I was a few months old, my parents went to the Temple and the priest picked the letter H, so my parents gave me a name starting with H."

# Nationality

All nations and peoples are unique and special. Having a nationality means that you have the protection and benefits of a country. It also means that you share a culture and a history with the other people in your country.

**Bangladesh** A young country, Bangladesh separated from Pakistan and finally became independent in 1971 after a long civil war. Today, Bangladesh is a vibrant country.

... Children participate in their country's "Say Yes for Children" campaign. The campaign aims to build support for the policies that will improve and protect the lives of children.

In **Northern Ireland** Stephen, Ruairi, and Connell are proud of their Irish culture and support their local Gaelic football team.

... Gaelic football is an ancient Irish sport where teams of players try to punch, bounce, or kick a ball into or over a net.

**Peru** The majority of people in Peru are Amerindian, descendants of the Incas who once ruled Peru.

... The Peruvian mountains are home to many millions of Amerindians who still speak the local language of Quechua and maintain a traditional way of life.

**Spain** Uxue lives in Santander, the capital city of a small province in northern Spain, called Cantabria. This region is very close to the northern provinces of the Basque Country, where the people have a completely unique language and culture.

... The regions of northern Spain are very different from those farther south. In Cantabria, it is more mountainous and not so sunny. It is beautiful.

**South Africa** Many different people live in South Africa. In addition to various local ethnic groups, South Africa is also home to people whose parents and grandparents emigrated from Europe and India.

... South Africa has 11 official languages. There are nine African languages, as well as Afrikaans and English, which were brought by the Dutch and British settlers who came in the 19th century.

# Najaha and Abdisukri

Najaha and Abdisukri are sister and brother. Their family came to the Netherlands from Somalia as refugees. They are now happy to think of themselves as Somali children living in the Netherlands.

ADJUSTING TO A NEW HOME
At school, Najaha and Abdisukri play with children from many different countries. Because they were young when they left Somalia, they have found it easy to adjust to life in the Netherlands.

...*"I like the Netherlands, but I don't like the weather. It's always raining and it's too cold!"*

Family photographs of Abdisukri and Najaha

## The Netherlands
The Dutch people who live in the Netherlands have a long history of welcoming refugees and people in need.

THE NETHERLANDS

GERMANY

BELGIUM

TWO LANGUAGES
Abdisukri and Najaha speak Somali when they are at home with their family, but most of the time they speak Dutch, the language of the Netherlands.

**SOCCER ACTION**
Abdisukri plays soccer with a famous soccer team near his home. It is called Willem II.

"Someday I want to be a professional soccer player with the Willem II soccer team like my favorite soccer player, Jatto Ceesay, who is from Gambia."

**DAILY PRAYERS**
Abdisukri and Najaha's family is Muslim. The whole family prays five times a day. They also go to the mosque together, where they meet some of their friends.

A plate with verses from the Koran

Abdisukri's soccer trophy

"I love to play soccer. My coach calls me Abdi and says he is very proud of me."

**SCHOOL TIME**
Najaha enjoys mathematics, reading, writing stories – and going to the amusement park! Study is important to Najaha because she wants to become a lawyer.

"I don't have any best friends. All my friends are my best friends."

Najaha's school books

"Our favorite food is samosas."

**FAVORITE FOOD**
At home, the family eats Somali food. *Samosas* are fried pancakes stuffed with meat and vegetables.

# Religion

Each religion means something very special to those who practice it. That is why it is important that no one is prevented from following a religion or faith.

Jewish *Torah* scroll and pointer     Tibetan Buddhist prayer wheel

**South Korea** Eyes shut to help their concentration, these children pray during Sunday school at a large Pentecostal church.

. . . In South Korea, about half the people are Christian and half are Buddhist.

**Myanmar** At the *shinbyu* ceremony, boys enter a Buddhist monastery for a short time. When they are older, they may decide to become monks.

**US** These girls are singing in a Gospel church choir. Gospel music is very lively. The singers often clap and sway while they are singing because they feel so excited about praising God.

. . . Gospel music has its roots in songs that Africans brought to America as slaves and sang while they worked.

Christian cross

Islamic tile

Sikh *nishan sahib* symbol

Ganesh, a Hindu god

RELIGION 111

**India** During a coming-of-age ceremony, young boys are given a sacred shirt and a thread to wear throughout their lives. This boy has now become a full member of the Parsi (Zoroastrian) community.

 The boys dress like royal princes in the days of the first Buddhist priests, more than 2,000 years ago. It is a proud day for their parents.

... The sacred thread, called the *kusti*, is wrapped three times around the waist. It represents three important things to remember – good thoughts, good deeds, and good words.

## A NEW LIFE

Eli's family spent two years arranging the move to Israel. Eli was scared but also curious about his new life.

# Eli

Eli came to Israel from Uzbekistan in the former Soviet Union. His family are Jewish, but Eli didn't know very much about Jewish beliefs or practices before he came to live in Israel.

## YEMIN ORDE

Many of Eli's classmates live at Yemin Orde Youth Village because they came to Israel without their parents. They learn about Judaism in school and also participate in Jewish activities outside school hours. Every Saturday, they celebrate *Shabbat*, the Jewish sabbath.

## Israel

Jews from all over the world have chosen to make Israel their home, though people of other faiths live in Israel, too.

 "My school is called Yemin Orde. I chose to come here so I could learn more about being Jewish."

## DIFFERENT BACKGROUNDS

Children at Yemin Orde come from more than 20 different countries including Ethiopia, Russia and the former Soviet Union, Brazil, Mexico, Colombia, Slovakia, Bosnia, Romania, Morocco, India, France, Italy, Great Britain, Martinique, and Israel!

> "It's really interesting meeting children from so many countries. We are all Jews, but we have different traditions, which we share with each other at Yemin Orde."

## TORAH

Eli studies the *Torah* – the Jewish holy book – in Hebrew, but he also has a translation into Russian to help him understand it better.

> "I like the special atmosphere on Shabbat. Sometimes I spend it with my family. We say some blessings at home, but I don't always go the synagogue."

*Torah*

*Kippa*

## PRAYER

There is a beautiful synagogue at Yemin Orde. To pray, Eli wears a skullcap called a *kippa*, a shawl called a *tallit*, and *tefillin*, which are little boxes containing verses from the *Torah*.

> "At school, we are encouraged but not forced to pray every day. I love finding out about my religion."

*Tefillin*, containing verses from the *Torah*

Every child has the right to free

# expression

opinions, contribution, respect,

# Saying and doing

Show how much you care and take an interest.
Expressing yourself means getting involved.
There are millions of ways to express yourself.
By expressing ourselves, we share things we like and dislike,
and how we think and feel. This is an opportunity
to learn about ourselves and others.

## participation, individuality, input

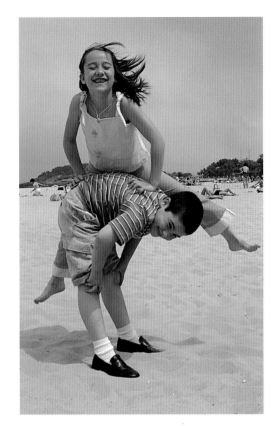

# Express yourself!

What **opinions** and **ideas** do you have? Do you think they are important? Well, you're right, they are important. Your **opinions** and **ideas** could change the world.

● The world is a **great**, **fun**, **scary**, **happy**, **sad**, **wonderful**, **exciting** place – but it could be better. Is there a problem in your school, town, country – or another country – that you think you could help solve?

● Everyone has the **right** to express an opinion, not just adults but children, too. Children who **cannot** express their opinions may feel frustrated about living in a world they can't change.

How many ways can you think of to express yourself?

● Children had their say at the UN Special Session on Children, held at the United Nations Headquarters in New York in May 2002. This was a chance for children from around the globe to talk to world leaders about issues affecting them.

# Take action
## and help make the world a better place by *expressing your opinions* and *participating*.

• **Think of** something you would like to see improved, or a problem you would like to see solved. It can be in your school, your city, or somewhere far away.

• **Think about** how you, as a child, can help solve that problem. For example, you might not have money, but you can encourage adults to give money to help.

• **Find out** all you can about that problem and tell your friends about it, too. You could make contact with groups that are already working to fix it.

• **Choose** one way to help. It can be a small thing, such as not wasting resources, or something bigger, such as starting your own organization.

## Getting adults to listen

Agree on a time with parents and teachers when they can listen to your concerns.

Try to bring along some facts to back up your opinions.

Allow your parents and teachers to respond to what you say.

Keep calm and treat people with respect.

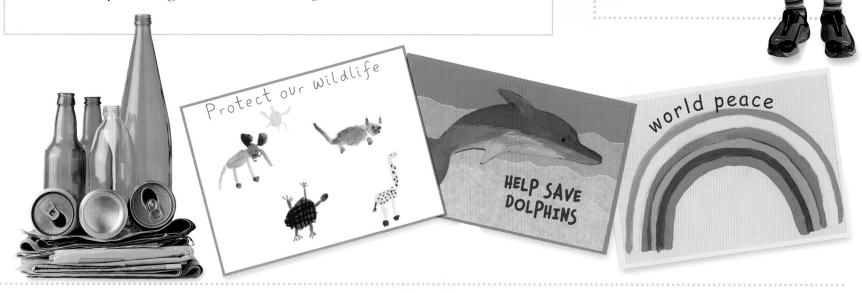

Protect our wildlife

HELP SAVE DOLPHINS

world peace

● **Creating** – draw, paint, sculpt, photograph, film, record, write. You can share what you make with others.

● **Participating** – recycle cans and bottles, pick up garbage in the streets, organize a clean-up in a local park.

● **Talking** – listen to what others have to say and tell them what you think. Try to see things differently.

● **Making friends** – every time you meet someone new, you can share new ideas and thoughts with that person.

● **Sharing** – other children may have the same problem or concern as you. Together, you could fix it.

# Freedom of expression

Human beings make speeches, write stories, paint pictures, compose and sing songs, perform dances, and act in plays. Sometimes we express ourselves because we have strong feelings or thoughts about something and we want to share them with other people. Sometimes we express ourselves because we feel we need to. Whatever the reason, self-expression is something to enjoy and take pride in.

**Brazil** These children, members of EDISCA dance school, discuss the production they are rehearsing. The show is about people who live in a garbage dump. The children in the dance company come from deprived communities themselves.

... Everyone has to work hard in a dance company. While this dancer balances in a strikingly graceful pose, another member works just as hard to support her there.

**Brazil** Diego stands in front of a mural he painted of Bob Marley, a Jamaican reggae musician. Artists frequently work alone, but a big work of art like this can involve many people.

. . . This mural means that Diego's work can be seen and appreciated by many people. It also makes the neighborhood much more colorful.

**Botswana** These girls are recording their discussion about AIDS for a radio program. AIDS is a big problem in Africa, and this program is a good way to get information about the disease out to young people.

**Bolivia** A young boy learns to play the guitar, a traditional instrument of the Andes. The musical notes are written down in his notebook.

. . . Once you can play an instrument, it's fun to play with a lot of other musicians.

. . . Self-expression includes art, dances, and music, but words are important, too. Children must speak out about things they care about or that affect them.

# Taralyn

"I play hand drums and clackers for traditional drumming, singing, and dancing. I think I'll always enjoy doing that."

Taralyn attends Chief Leschi School near Seattle. The Puyallup nation of Native Americans runs the school, but pupils come from more than 60 Native American nations. They study English, math, and many other subjects, as well as learning all about different tribal traditions.

## US

Before Europeans arrived in the US 400 years ago, the land was home to hundreds of Native American nations.

## LANGUAGES
Some children speak a Native American language, but classes are in English.

## SACRED LAND
The school is constructed around a sacred circle of land that stayed untouched throughout the building process. Students and teachers do not enter this area, but many school buildings look onto it.

"You can see Mount Rainier from our school. There are eagles that like to fly over our school. I think that is special too."

## CIRCLE TIME

Every day there is an opportunity for children to sing traditional songs, do some drumming, and learn about each other's nations during Circle Time.

... "I like Circle best because we get to sing, drum, and dance. Sometimes we also have special guests and storytelling."

... "Powwows are social celebrations. They don't belong to our historical tradition, but to that of the Plains tribes. We love to join in anyway."

## CULTURE DAY

The school holds an annual celebration of Native American traditions. Local people are invited to join in the dancing. All year, the children make gifts, which they finally give away during Culture Day.

## TOTEM POLE

There are several totem poles on the school grounds. Each one illustrates a particular legend and took months to carve.

... "In the main entrance to our school, we have a totem pole that tells how the Puyallup River was formed by two black whales after a great flood."

## SALMON FEAST

Living near the coast, the Puyallup nation traditionally enjoyed salmon as one of its staple foods. There's always a big salmon barbecue on Culture Day.

# Every child deserves a happy

# life

## dreams, wishes, ambitions, goals,

# Aim high!
## The future is in your hands.
You can make a better world.

What are your wishes for the future?

All around the world, children like you are working to improve their communities. If we all work together, we can create a world where there is a happy life for everyone.

## achievements, hope, happiness

# Sibasish

The World Health Organization, UNICEF, and other partners are trying to wipe out polio. Sibasish is a team leader in a project that teaches people living in slums in Kolkata (Calcutta), India, about the disease and encourages families to vaccinate their children against it.

## India

More than a billion people live in India, making it the world's second most populated country. The climate ranges from tropical monsoon in the south to temperate in the north.

## POLIO KILLS

A highly infectious disease, polio mostly affects poor children under five years old. Polio can be transmitted through food or water. It starts with the same symptoms as the flu, but it sometimes leads to paralysis and, rarely, death.

"We walk down the streets with posters. Mine says: 'Get vaccinated and lead a good life.' We play music and sing songs to get the message out."

Polio vaccine

## HOUSE TO HOUSE

Sibasish talks about polio and invites people to attend an immunization day when their children can be vaccinated. Most are very happy to be protected against the disease and don't need much persuasion.

"We go on campaigns three times a week to all the homes with children under five. We teach people about polio and the importance of the vaccination."

## THE CAMPAIGN AGAINST POLIO

It is a privilege to be involved in the campaign. Local children train as campaigners each year. In addition to learning about polio, they learn to be good communicators and leaders.

"Sometimes we go to people who are not in a good mood and they throw us out. We don't give up. Instead, we go back again a day or two later when they have calmed down and tell them about polio."

Colorful charts

Campaign bag

"Each child campaigner gets a special bag. We have fun making charts and posters, which we carry in these bags and use when we campaign."

## IMMUNIZATION DAY

The work pays off on immunization day. The campaigners do a final round, making sure that parents are taking their children to be vaccinated.

"We want a world free from polio."

"I want to do good for other human beings and give every child a better tomorrow."

## TAKING THE VACCINE

A health worker gives a child the vaccine. It is usually two drops of liquid on the tongue. To be completely effective, four separate doses must be taken.

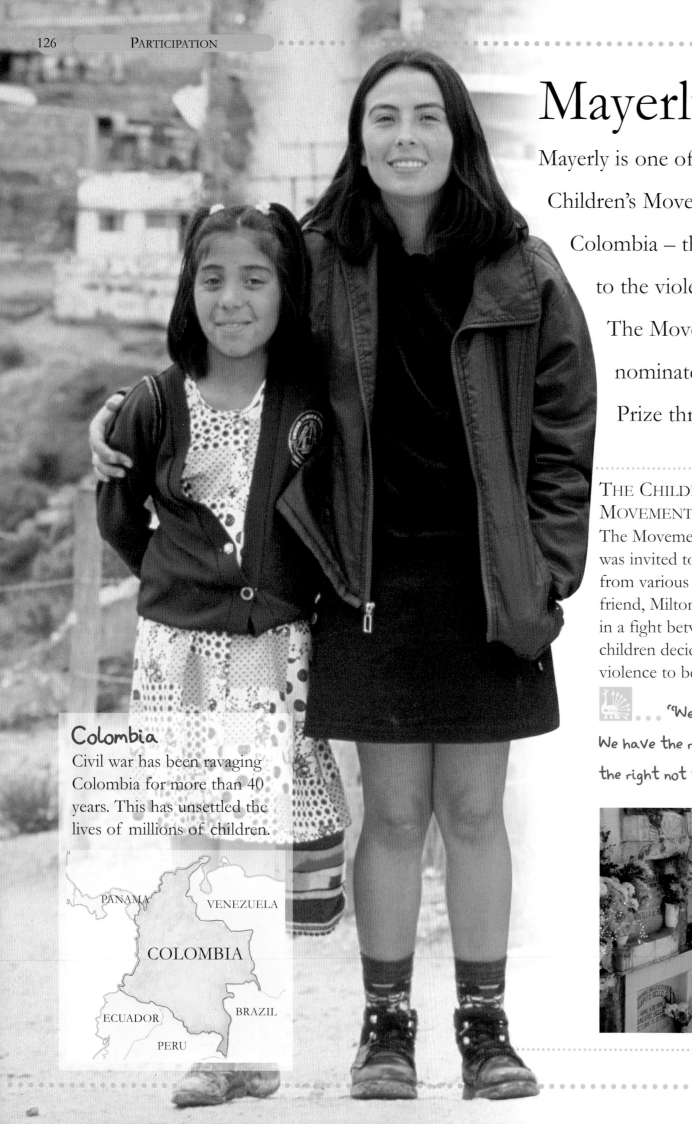

# Mayerly

Mayerly is one of the leaders of the Children's Movement for Peace in Colombia – the children's response to the violence in their country. The Movement has been nominated for a Nobel Peace Prize three times.

## THE CHILDREN'S MOVEMENT FOR PEACE

The Movement began when Mayerly was invited to a meeting with children from various organizations. Her best friend, Milton, had recently been killed in a fight between youth gangs. The children decided it was time for the violence to be stopped.

*"We are tired of violence. We have the right to be children, and the right not to be afraid to go out."*

## Colombia

Civil war has been ravaging Colombia for more than 40 years. This has unsettled the lives of millions of children.

PANAMA     VENEZUELA

COLOMBIA

ECUADOR          BRAZIL

PERU

### LEARNING ABOUT PEACE

The symbol of the Children's Movement for Peace is the white hand seen on books, T-shirts, and banners. The Movement includes more than 100,000 children. They play games and support each other instead of joining violent gangs and becoming involved with weapons and drugs.

 . . . "The white hand means no to violence."

### PEACEBUILDERS

The Movement believes that Colombia's children deserve the right to live, the right to peace, the right to love, and the right to safety for themselves and their families. Parades like these have helped the government ban the recruitment of children under the age of 18 into the Colombian army.

. . . The banner proclaims "I am a peacebuilder" – the dove of peace flies over the Colombian flag.

### MAYERLY'S MOM

Mayerly's parents were worried that she might be harmed for her involvement in the Movement. Now they are very proud of their daughter.

. . . "We are convincing children in our schools and people in our neighorhoods that this is the way to a better future. No one can kill 10 million Colombians who speak about peace."

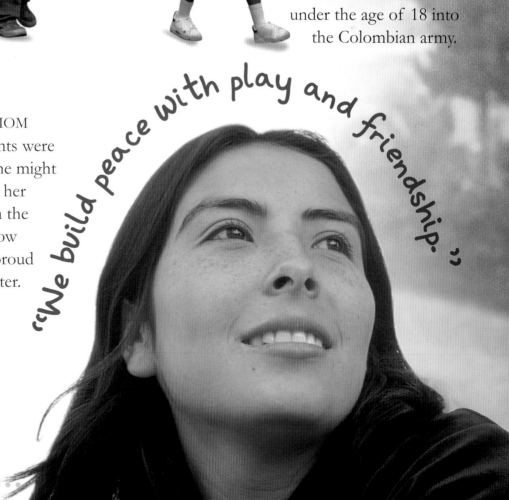

"We build peace with play and friendship."

# Index

# Acknowledgments

**DK would like to thank:**

All the children and their parents who participated in the book, particularly: Anita McDaniel; Jacqueline Mliswa; and Raili Jones.

The staff of UNICEF and the staff of UNICEF National Committees in all the countries we visited and the people working with them, particularly: Sara Cameron, Siddharth Dube, Hirut Gebre-Egziabher, Patricia Lone, Jan Mun, Tina Omari, Hashi Roberts, Ellen Tolmie, Nicole Toutounji (New York); Chulho Hyun (Afghanistan); Naseem-Ur Rehman (Bangladesh); Rochita Talukdar (India); Susan Aitkin (Laos); Bert Tielemans (Netherlands); Monica Awad (Occupied Palestinian Territory); Cyriaque Ngoboka (Rwanda); Donald Robertshaw (Sierra Leone); Nance Webber (Sudan); Andy Bool (UK); Patrick Fruchet (Yugoslavia).

All of the schools, teachers, and organizations who assisted us, particularly: Deborah Allen, Tami Cooper, Erika Hope (Chief Leschi School); Laura Buller (US consultant); Tony Ackerman (Ellerton School); Michelle Berriedale-Johnson (Allergy Action); Lewsey Park Pool (UK); Planet Ice (UK); Sharon Knight (Wilbury Junior School, Letchworth, UK); Lisa Leblanc (Special Olympics, Atlanta, Georgia); Sacha Kamau and Zoe Horner (The Travel Company, London); Tamsin Maunder (WaterAid); Chaim Peri, Susan Weijel (Yemin Orde, Israel); Cristina and Alex Zampalo.

All of the people at Dorling Kindersley, particularly: Jacqueline Gooden, Tory Gordon-Harris, Cheryl Telfer (design assistance); Abbie Collinson (map artworks); Penny Arlon, Caroline Bingham, Simon Holland, Rebecca Knowles, Cynthia O'Neill (editorial assistance); Jane Oliver-Jedrzejak (jacket editor); Jenny Cavill, Kristen L'huede, Mariza O'Keeffe (administration); David Roberts (cartography); Alex Kirkham (licensing); Sarah Mills, Gemma Woodward, Hayley Smith, Claire Bowers (picture library); Rosie Adams (DK Australia); Shuka Jain, Kiran Mohan (photography coordination, DK India).

Chris Bernstein (index); Lorrie Mack (proofreading).

The photographers: Shome Basu (India), Andy Crawford (Netherlands, Spain, UK, US), Jim Holmes (Laos), Roger Lemoyne (Israel, Occupied Palestinian Territory), Leon Mead (Australia), Shehzad Noorani (Bangladesh, Sudan, Yugoslavia), Rod Shone (UK), Jon Spaull (Rwanda, Sierra Leone), Asad Zaidi (Afghanistan).

The publisher would like to thank the following for their kind permission to reproduce their photographs:

a=above; b=below; c=center; l=left; r=right; t=top;

**Andes Press Agency:** 56bl, 57bl, 75bc, 90bl, 90br, 114bc; Lisa Payne 107tr; Carlos Reyes-Manzo 60tr, 100bl; **Art Directors & TRIP:** 30bl; H Rogers 111tc; **John Birdsall Photo Library:** 71cl; **Corbis:** 30-31, 51tr, 74br, 77, 84tr, 90, 91bl, 103tr, 110bl, 115bc; Abbie Enoch 30bc; Owen Franken 19c; Julie Houck 39bc; Richard Hutchings 22tr; Joel W Rogers 39br; Michael S Yamashita 18br; **Jane Cumberbatch:** 45tr, 46br; **Earth Images:** 12tr; **Getty Images:** 69tr, 90c; **Getty Images News Service:** 68tl, 82-3, 100-1; Don Smetzer 93br; **Glasgow Museum:** 103bc; **Hutchison Library:** 71tr, 71cr; **Images Of Africa Photobank:** 30bl; **Impact Photos:** 122-123; **Jewish Museum:** 110tr; **Joods Historisch Museum:** 102br; **Magnum:** 4tc, 4tr, 5tr, 8tr, 23tc, 23tr, 23r, 30bc, 44tl, 44tr, 44tcl, 44tcr, 45tl, 45tcl, 46bl, 46bc, 47bl, 47bc, 56bc, 56br, 57bc, 57br, 64tl, 64tc, 66bl, 66bc, 66br, 67bl, 67bc, 70cr, 74bc, 75bl, 75br, 76tl, 83bc, 91br, 94tr, 94cr, 94br, 94l, 95bl, 100bc, 101bl, 101br, 110cl, 110-1, 111cr; Daniel Alan Harvey 98tc1, 114br; Steve Moss 122br; **Masterfile UK:** 66-7; **Network Photographers Ltd.:** Jenny Matthews 67br; **Panos Pictures:** 71bl; **Pictorial Press Ltd:** 65tcl; **Pictor International:** 11br, 58, 74-5, 91bc; **Powell Cotton Museum:** 102bl; **Powerstock Photolibrary:** 18-19; **Save the Children:** 19bl; Neil Cooper 47br; **Science Photo Library:** 38-9; **Still Pictures:** 87c; Shehzad Noorani 10bl, 10br; Hirimui Schwarzbach 10bc; **Peter Stone:** 65tr; © **UNICEF:** Blid Alsbirk 15r, 95bl; Cindy Andrew 18c; Patricio Baeza 119br; Alejandro Balaguer 61bl, 76cr; David Barbour 61br; Liza Barrie 93tl; Radhika Chalasani 87br,123r; Franck Charton 64tr, 74l; John Chiasson 122l; Stephanie Colvey 41cl; Donna DeCesare 6bc, 99br, 126c, 127br; Lauren Goodsmith 64ctl, 79cl, 79bl; Jeremy Horner 50cl, 50bl, 78c, 98tr, 115r, 126br, 127tl, 127tr, 127c, 127cr, 127bl; Altaf Hossain 106c; Roger Lemoyne 14c, 14l, 22bl, 30tr, 30br, 36c, 36l, 37r, 39br, 41bc, 65tl, 82l, 82c, 82r, 83l, 95c, left back end paper; Stevie Mann 65tc, 86c, 86t, 86bl, 86br; Susan Markisz 116bc; Ruby Mera 98tcr, 114bl; Shehzad Noorani 9tr, 41ct, 50tr, 50br, 61tl; Giacomo Pirozzi 8tl, 8ctl, 8tcr, 9tc, 11l, 23r, 28tr, 40l, 41cr, 51r, 60bc, 61cr, 70bl, 79bl, 85tr, 87t, 99tr, 101c, 107br, 115br, 119bl; Betty Press 87cl; Nicole Toutounji 83r, 84bc, 85bc; Claudio Versiani 99tcl, 99tcr, 118c, 118tr, 119tl.

Jacket: **Corbis:** Tim Page front cl; **Getty Images:** Brian Bailey front tll; Wayne Eastep front trr; Dan Kenyon front bl; David Roth front br; **Barnabas & Anabel Kindersley:** back tl, tr, cl, cr, front b; **Magnum:** Abbas front tl; Ian Berry front tcr, tcrr; Harry Gruyaert front tc, Peter Marlow front bc; Chris Steele-Perkins front cr; **The Photographers' Library:** inside back; **Planetary Visions:** inside front bl; **Save the Children:** back bl, bcr; Neil Cooper back br; **Still Pictures:** Hirimui Schwarzbach spine t; © **UNICEF:** Radhika Chalasani back bcl; Nancy McGirr front tr.

All other images © Dorling Kindersley.

For further information see: www.dkimages.com